Industrial architecture

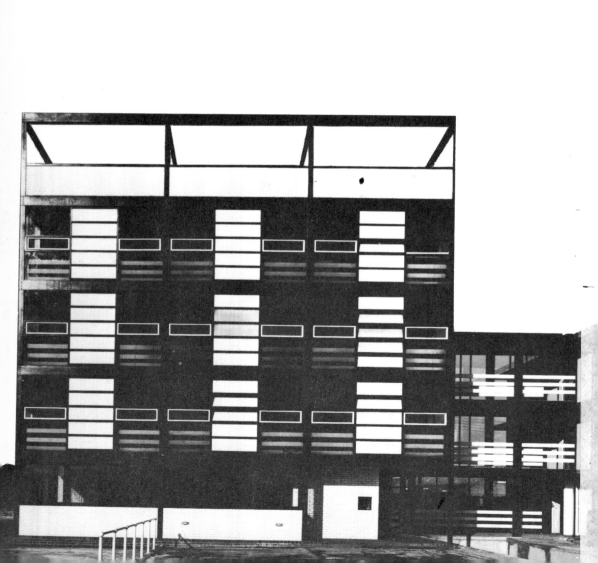

Industrial architecture

A survey of factory building

John Winter

Studio Vista London

Back cover illustrations:

Print of early cotton mill
(Photograph - Eric de Maré)
Reliance Controls, Swindon
Architects: Team 4
(Photograph - Norman Foster)

725·4

© John Winter 1970
First published in Great Britain 1970
by Studio Vista Limited, Blue Star House,
Highgate Hill, London N19
Set in Plantin 11 pt, 1 pt leaded
Printed in the Netherlands
by N.V. Grafische Industrie Haarlem, Holland
SBN 289 79773 X

Contents

Introduction

Many books have been written about the history of architecture, but almost all concern themselves with buildings remote from our ordinary lives; in consequence most of us have a fairly accurate mental picture of an English Gothic cathedral or an American colonial country house, but cannot imagine the building where Model T Fords were made.

Until recently architects had a similar blind spot, and the logical thought behind the development of the factory throughout the eighteenth and nineteenth centuries was achieved without them. The creative minds during this period were the mill engineers, who, unhampered by architectural conventions, invented metal skeleton construction and the all-glass wall, pioneered artificial heating and lighting, giving us the technological and aesthetic base for the architecture of our own day.

In this century the image of the factory has changed from the 'dark Satanic mill' to the building whose products emerge 'factory fresh', and the best new factories are among the freshest products of all.

1 The milling of corn

The grinding of corn to make flour has been a basic and extensive part of our civilization for ten thousand years; successive cultures have sought ways of relieving the laborious work involved, and flour milling was probably the first industry to use animal power. It was the first to use wind power, probably the first to use water power and it was certainly the first to use the steam engine.

We know that the pestle and mortar of the neolithic woman had been superseded by the quern in pre-dynastic Egypt; in classical Greece the hand-turned rotary mill was in use and the Roman legions spread its use from the Persian Gulf to Hadrian's Wall. The rotary mill consisted of two grooved stones, the lower one fixed and the upper one revolving to grind the corn, an arrangement which survived unchanged until the invention of horizontal roller grinders in Hungary in the nineteenth century. But although the grinding mechanism remained unchanged for over two thousand years, the motive power was continuously varied; the ancient Romans, with abundant slave labour, were generally content with hand milling, but even they sometimes used the horse gin, the donkey treadmill or the water-wheel.

Windmills

Wind-driven prayer wheels are of great antiquity in the East, and in Persia during the seventh century the idea was adapted to the more mundane use of driving a water scoop for land irrigation, and soon afterwards for corn milling. The Persians did not have gears so the windmill sails and the grindstone were on the same vertical axle, with the grindstones on the upper floor and the sails on the open ground floor.

During the early twelfth century, knowledge of the windmill came to Europe, and knowledge of gearing obtained from watermills enabled the axle of the sails to be placed horizontally, giving us the windmill as we know it. This arrangement was much more efficient and gave far greater power, but required the sails to be turned to face into the wind. In the Aegean, simple windmills were built facing the prevailing wind; they had thatched conical roofs and canvas sails which wound round their spars like roller reefing on a yacht. In Western Europe the more sophisticated post mill was evolved. This mill had a timber structure which carried the sails and contained all the mechanisms; it swivelled on a wooden post and the miller turned it to face the wind by pushing the long tail-pole: many examples, such as Saxtead Green Mill in Essex still remain in good order. However to support a mill and its sails on a single post is structurally difficult, very heavy timbers being needed to prevent the wind from blowing it over. So ingenious minds sought ways of making just the cap carrying the sails revolve, keeping the main part of the mill stationary: the Dutch solved this in 1430 with the hollow post mill where the drive was transmitted down the centre of the hollow timber cylinder on which the cap revolved. By this date the English had evolved mills where the timber cap revolved on rollers on top of a timber polygonal structure (smock mill) or a brick cylinder (tower mill).

1 Old and new industrial buildings in Lincolnshire, England. Tower mill and electricity generating station (Photo – Eric de Maré)

It is the tower mill which is typical of England, but before it reached perfection two tedious manual operations had to be eliminated. In the early tower mills the miller had to watch for any change in direction or velocity of the wind. If there was a change in direction he had to go outside and push the tail-pole so that the cap revolved to face the sails into the wind again; and if there was a significant change in the velocity of the wind he had to alter his spread of canvas. In 1745 Edward Lee invented the fantail, a fan at right angles to and directly behind the main sails. If the fantail was not parallel to the wind it would revolve, driving a rod with a gear and ratchet in the cap of the mill to turn it automatically to the correct position. Automatic turning into the wind had been achieved by one man; automatic sail adjustment required the skill of several inventors — first Andrew Meikle who in 1772 invented the 'spring sail' with hinged slats linked together like a Venetian blind; then Captain Cooper, who in 1789 patented the 'roller reefing sail' where, for the first time, the spread of canvas could be altered without stopping the mill; and finally William Cubitt, who, in 1807, produced his 'patent sail' taking items from both the previous inventions and coupling them with a control system of iron bars in front of the sail. Cooke's mill at Stalham, Norfolk, was the first to have patent sails, and was. soon followed by another at nearby Horning which took the next step forward by having iron shutters.

Tower mills were often of great size: Southtown Mill, Great Yarmouth, was 102 feet high, and the mill still standing at Sutton, Norfolk is 80 feet high. The brick drum was tapered for stability, to provide larger rooms at the bottom and a good air flow at the top, and the windows were often positioned at random so as to avoid lines of weakness in the structure. The cap was of wood, and in contrast to the severe brickwork below, it was often fancifully shaped — like an upturned boat in Norfolk or as an onion dome in Lincolnshire.

A typical tower mill generated about ten horsepower from its sails which were mounted on an axle slightly tilted to avoid striking the brickwork below; this axle would have been of oak, perhaps 24 ft long and 10 in. diameter, until the middle of the eighteenth century when Smeaton (of Eddystone Lighthouse fame) published his investigations into windmills and introduced iron which enabled much lighter drives to be used. The axle would drive a vertical shaft through bevel gears and this shaft would take the power down into the brick cylinder and the great spur wheel, some 10 feet in diameter, which in turn would drive two, three or four vertical shafts revolving the millstones. Further gearing would operate the sack hoist, the bolters and other ancillary machinery.

Most windmills were used to power corn mills, but many were used to pump the water from the English fens and the Dutch polders. In the early stages of the industrial revolution they offered, for two brief decades, a serious competitor to the water wheel for driving textile mills but wind proved a less steady power source than the flow of a river.

In the late nineteenth century windmills were still being built in England, but when steam engines and later portable diesel motors became available these sources of power were adapted by the millers to drive their mills, so the sails decayed although the mills survived. Finally, with most of the corn imported from abroad, great mills were established at the English ports, and the economics of the small country mill ceased to be viable.

Watermills

The waterwheel as a power source is much older than the windmill, and was in use in China in 2200 BC. Vitruvius writing in Rome at about the time of Christ describes undershot wheels which 'accomplish the necessary work through being turned by the mere impulse of the river, without any treading on the part of the workmen'. He then describes how 'a drum with teeth is fixed into one end of the axle; it is set vertically on its edge and turns in the same plane as the wheel. Next to this larger drum there is a smaller one, also with teeth, but set horizontally, and this is attached to the millstone. Thus the teeth of the drum which is fixed to the axle make the teeth of the horizontal drum move and cause the mill to turn. A hopper hanging over this contrivance supplies the mill with corn, and the meal is produced by the same revolution.' The method remained unchanged for nearly 2000 years, except for the addition of controls. Roman organization built larger watermills than any later time, and we know of a fourth century mill near Arles which had sixteen overshot wheels each driving a pair of millstones with a total capacity of grinding three tons of corn an hour.

With the passing of slavery, milling by hand quern almost disappeared, and the simultaneous loss of Roman organization in Western Europe meant that each hamlet had to have its own mill. The first record of a watermill in England is the granting of the use of a mill to a monastery near Dover by Ethelberg of Kent in 762 and in the Middle Ages there were some 20000 watermills in use in England. The millers were the most independent men of the time as they were outside the feudal system of land tenure and lived by keeping a percentage, usually five per cent, of the corn they ground.

The typical English watermill had a brick base and timber upper-works, and it was either placed alongside the river with an undershot wheel dipped in the water, or it straddled the river and had an overshot or a breast wheel incorporated within it. Smeaton was as interested in waterwheels as he was in windmills, and in 1759 he put the study on a scientific basis and proved mathematically the superiority of the overshot wheel; he raised the power of waterwheels from ten to fifty horsepower and changed the cog wheels from applewood to iron.

Most mills are the product of continual alteration and improvement, but Horstead Mill, Norfolk, was built all at one time and serves as an example of the immediately post-Smeaton mill. Locks were built at Horstead, eight miles north of Norwich in 1779 to make the River Bure navigable to Aylsham. This had the effect of concentrating a five-foot change of water level and John Colls and Palmer Watts decided to rebuild their mill

2 Coggeshall Mill, Essex. Typical East Anglian watermill with timber upper works. It is still working by waterpower and grinding animal feeding stuffs (Photo – Eric de Maré)

to take advantage of this and their building was completed in 1789. By the standards of the day it was a large mill, for Norfolk was a wheat growing county. The building was designed to handle all the traffic without confusion, two locums — those overhanging gabled hoists so typical of mill buildings — hung over the water to enable the sailing wherries to be unloaded and the ground floor was arcaded so that farm carts could drive through and be loaded under cover. Corn from the boats was taken up by power hoist through leather-hinged flaps in the locum floor and stored on

3 Horstead Mill, Norfolk, England, 1789. The projecting gables, called 'locums' are for hoisting the grain from boats to the top floor (Photo – Birkin Haward)

the top floor which was big enough to contain 7000 sacks; this floor was well cross-ventilated to dry the corn and there were traps in the floor to feed the corn into the bins of the floor below. From these bins the corn flowed into the hoppers above the three grinding stones on the first floor and after grinding the flour travelled, again by gravity, into the sacks on the ground floor. In the river a breast wheel 15 ft diameter, 7 ft 6 in. wide drove a vertical shaft which had a great spur wheel, 9 ft diameter, placed just under the ground floor ceiling, driving the three millstones. The vertical shaft, which was of oak, 10 in. diameter and 14 ft long, extended up to the ceiling of the first floor and drove ancilliary machinery and hoists from gears at first floor ceiling level. Flour and water must not mix and the construction and appearance of the building clearly demonstrated which part belonged to flour and which to water: the lower part was of brick which is unaffected by water and strong enough to take wheel bearings and the continual buffeting of farm carts. The walls were 18 in. thick and the mill was 106 ft long and 26 ft wide, with a central row of posts and a further 14 ft of width under the arcade. The upper portion was of timber with a characteristic Norfolk pantile and barge boarded roof. The timber siding took no stress (as would have been usual in nineteenth century American construction), hence heavy timbers and diagonals were present everywhere, with iron straps to obviate the complicated carpentry involved in jointing; timber was especially preferred for mills as there is less damp and condensation than with other building materials. The brick ground floor, expressed in the arches, was on a ten-foot module, whereas the timber structure above was on an eight-foot module, clearly expressed in the gabled roof, and this lack of alignment gave the building a relaxed, almost casual look. Exactly a century after its completion a turbine was installed to drive horizontal roller grinders, and standby electric power was introduced in 1930. Horstead Mill was destroyed by fire in 1963.

After Smeaton the development of waterwheels was taken up by the French. Poncelet in 1824 improved the undershot wheel by sloping the sluice to increase the speed of running water and by curving the blades on the wheel; one of his wheels in Spain generated one hundred and fifty horsepower from a six-foot drop in water level. At the same time another Frenchman, Benoit Fourneyron evolved the turbine which generated more power from the same flow of water, and turbines replaced waterwheels in many English mills. An American, Oliver Evans, developed the waterwheel to its furthest extent, but by this time the steam engine was proving more efficient and Evans' work is the swan song of the waterwheel technique.

4 Interior of Horstead Mill (Photo – Birkin Haward)

Steam-driven mills

Savery's first practical steam engine was working in 1698 and by 1712 Newcomen had made a steam engine which was commercially sound for pumping water out of mines and was made in considerable numbers for that purpose. However, pumping needs a reciprocating motion, and the rotary motion needed to drive machinery was not available until Boulton and Watt put 'sun and planet' gearing on an engine in 1784 and converted the up and down motion of the piston arm to a revolving shaft and flywheel.

Because the early steam engines could pump water but not drive shafts, and because the steam engine arrived at a time when millwrights thought in terms of waterpower, there was a curious transitional period when steam engines were used to pump water from the tail race to the head race of a mill, and the water then drove a traditional waterwheel. An example of this intermediate stage in the development of the steam-powered corn mill was built by Smeaton in 1781. This mill ground ninety tons of corn a week in the navy victualling yard at Deptford. It was powered by a waterwheel, but all the waterworks were artificial, water being pumped from the lower level to the higher by a Newcomen engine.

In 1784 Boulton and Watt produced the first steam engine giving rotary drive, and before the engine was even tested Samuel Wyatt started to build the great Albion Mill on London's South Bank. At that time there were some five hundred flour mills in London, driven by water, wind or horse gin, and the largest of them had four grinding wheels. For Albion Mill, Wyatt planned thirty wheels, each much larger than those normally used, and by changing the wheels to avoid overheating he intended to run them day and night; the motive power was to come from three Boulton and Watt engines driving all-iron gearing, and the vast scale of the enterprise was as novel as the power source. The building itself was very direct and rather beautiful. It had brick exterior walls with great arched openings and timber posts and floors internally, and so structurally it was similar to John Lombe's Derby Silk Mill of sixty-five years before, but alas! unlike his friend William Strutt of Derby, Wyatt did not develop a technique of fire-proof construction and the great Albion Mill was gutted by fire within five years of its completion. We are told that the crowd cheered the flames as they feared that such an efficient mill would cause unemployment, and Samuel Wyatt and the other promoters were relieved for precisely the opposite reason — the mill had never been a commercial success and they were glad to be rid of it.

The English flour millers seem to have taken fright at the sad fate of Albion Mill, for although the nineteenth century millers added steam engines to the old country mills, as at Chilham in Kent and Fakenham in Norfolk, it was left to the textile mills to develop the steam-powered factory.

5 Albion Mill, Southwark, London, built in 1786 and destroyed by fire in 1791. It was the first mill to be powered by a rotary steam engine and the lower picture **6**, a cartoon of the time, shows the owners of windmills dancing with joy at its destruction. The sign reads 'Success to the Mills of Albion, but no Albion Mills' (Pictures – Fire Protection Association)

6

7 Chilham Mill, Kent, England, an old water powered mill converted to steam. Both sources of power are now defunct (Photo – Eric de Maré)

8 Waterwheels

a Undershot wheels, oldest and least efficient
b Poncelet wheel, like the undershot, but velocity of water increased by a sluice
c Overshot wheel. Proved by Smeaton to be the most efficient
d Pitch-back wheel: the advantage was that water in the tail race ran with the wheel, not against it as with the overshot
e Breast wheel, the type used at Horstead Mill
f Turbine — coming late in the water power period, the turbine proved most efficient of all. It was completely immersed in the water and placed horizontally; the shaded central part was fixed, the outer part revolved

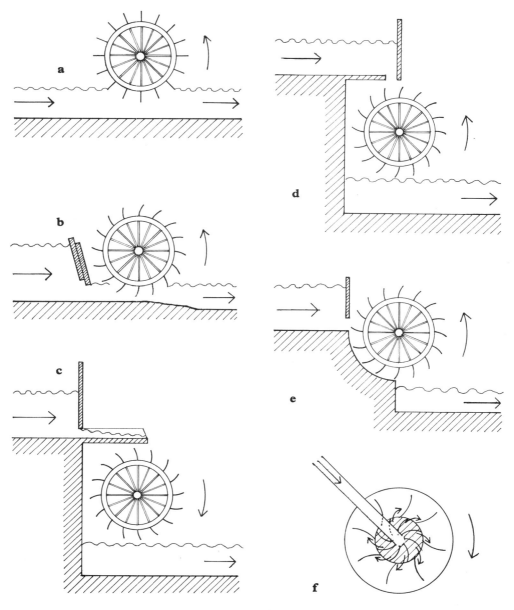

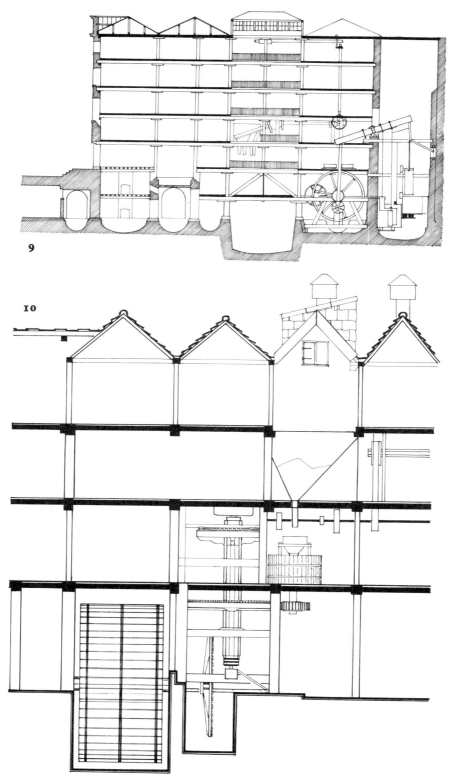

9

10

9-12 Power sources and transmission

---

9 Albion Mill, 1786. Boulton and Watt steam engine drives iron shaft system to millstones
10 Horstead Mill, 1789. 15 ft diameter breast wheel drives timber shaft to millstones
11 North Mill, Belper, England, 1803. 18 ft diameter water wheel drives iron gearing to give overhead shafting throughout the mill to power the frames. The top floor has no power as it served as a schoolroom where the young workers had to attend on Sundays
12 *overpage*

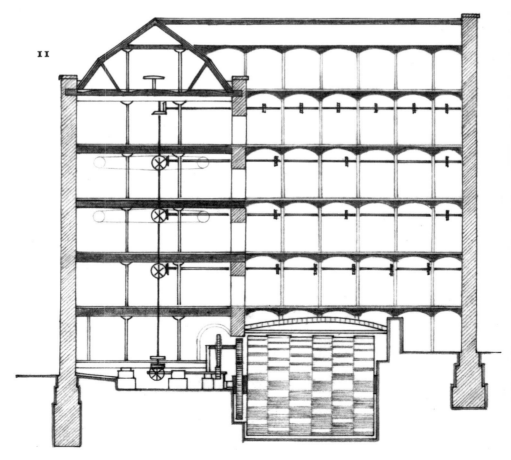

11

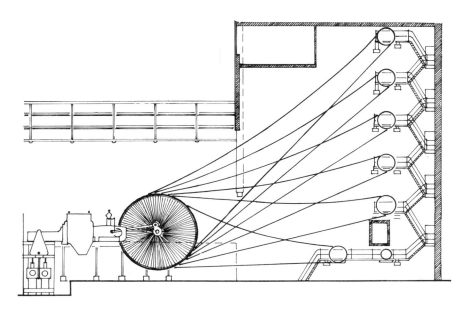

12 Cotton mill of the 1870s. Horizontal steam engine drives flywheel some 30ft in diameter. This flywheel is grooved to take about thirty ropes which drive a pulley on each floor; these pulleys are attached to the ends of the overhead shafts which drive the mules. Iron stairs and galleries give access to the pulleys, as the ropes often break

One nineteenth century flour mill is of great significance as it has a claim to being the first building where all the vertical loads are carried on an iron structure. This was a mill built by Fairbairn in 1840. It was of two storeys, with outside walls of iron plates, strengthened by hollow iron pilasters; it was first erected in Fairbairn's Millwall yard, then dismantled and shipped to Istanbul. Transverse loads and machinery shafts were taken on a brick cross wall, so the true iron frame was not yet perfected.

2 Water power and textiles

The developments in Britain during the period 1760-1820 were of an importance comparable with the first cultivation of crops or the domestication of animals. At the beginning of the period the English village was self-sufficient with a few cottage industries; by 1820 goods were made by machines in factories and trade was on a world scale.

It was the cotton industry that led the way.

Technical background

In mid-eighteenth century England weaving was a cottage industry: it employed the farm worker in his spare time and his wife and children all day. By 1760 Kay's flying shuttle was in general use and made the weavers more productive, while the introduction of Paul's carding machine at the same time caused a great bottleneck in spinning. Weavers were limited by the amount of yarn available and the yarn from the hand-operated spinning wheels was not only inadequate in quantity, it was of such poor quality that linen had to be used for the warp of the woven cloth.

In 1769 Arkwright patented his 'water-frame' spinning machine which enabled yarn to be spun by machinery. It required either horsepower or water power to drive it, so spinning as a cottage industry was doomed. The need for power took industries into factories, and as water power was soon found to be the most economical the early factories were built along fast-flowing watercourses, which were often situated in remote places. Arkwright's water-frame was followed in the next year by Hargreaves' patent for his 'spinning Jenny' which enabled the spinning of yarn to be carried out on a larger scale by a simpler machine. In 1779 Crompton brought the spinning machine to perfection with his 'mule'. In 1787 Cartwright installed power looms in a mill in Doncaster, but this venture was not successful and the cottage weavers enjoyed boom conditions until power weaving became common in the nineteenth century.

The inventiveness of the English cotton makers would have led them to outrun supplies had it not coincided with a great improvement in cotton supplies from the southern states of the young American Republic. The use of Eli Whitney's cotton gin on the great slave plantations revolutionized the process, and production of raw American cotton rose fifty-fold in the period 1780–1840.

The first generation cotton mills

In 1718 Christopher Wren, Nicholas Hawksmoor and John Vanbrugh were the key figures on the English architectural scene, designing masterly buildings for church and landowner, unaware that a building then under construction by the river Derwent might seem to future generations to have more relevance than all the majesty of the English Baroque. For in that year John Lombe built a silk mill in Derby which is not only the ancestor of all our factories, but is also the great-grandfather of the regular framed skeleton construction upon which the best modern buildings depend. Demolished in this century, and so far as I know never photographed, we do not know much about this pioneer building, but we do know that it was thirty-nine ft wide with regularly spaced wood pillars down the centre, one hundred and ten ft long and five storeys high with the outer wall in masonry containing four hundred and sixty-eight windows! It is amazing how little industrial buildings changed in the next two hundred years, for with only minor alterations John Lombe's building set the style for the first generation textile mills on the Derwent and the Frome, for the later mills of Lancashire and New England and indeed for most factory buildings, until Albert Kahn thought out the problem anew in the 1920s. In the two hundred years after 1718 the factory changed less than other building types, sure indication not only of the conservatism of factory builders, but also of the remarkable prescience of the Derby silk mill, completed just a decade

13 Conjectural restoration of John Lombe's Silk Mill of 1718. John Lombe had learnt about silk throwing and waterwheels in Italy and this knowledge was the basis on which he built the first real factory

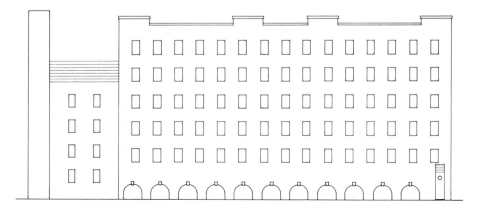

after St Paul's Cathedral.

John Lombe obtained much of his know-how from Italy and is responsible for bringing to England the far superior Italian knowledge of both silk throwing and of water power, and so starting English industry on its one hundred and fifty years of supremacy. His mill had an 18 ft diameter undershot water wheel which drove no fewer than 26000 machine wheels, so the factory arrived fully grown.

The Derby mill had been a one-off building, but with the invention of Arkwright's water-frame the factory system came to stay. As it was his patent during the 1770s and early 1780s, it is to his licensees that we must look for the early factories — Arkwright, Strutt and Need's mill at Cromford of 1771, Arkwright and Strutt's mill at Belper of 1776, Arkwright, Simpson and Whitenburgh's mill at Manchester of 1780 and Arkwright and David Dale's mill at New Lanark of 1784.

Arkwright was a man of humble origin who rose to immense wealth; he had been apprenticed to a barber in Preston, but devoted his energies to inventing and improving the inventions of others, and after he patented the water-frame he found no difficulty in finding financial backers. Arkwright's competitor, Hargreaves, had his Lancashire workshop destroyed by Luddites in 1767, and as a result both Arkwright and Hargreaves moved to Nottingham which they felt would be safer. Arkwright's first factory was built in Nottingham in 1769, it employed some three hundred people and was probably four storeys high; the motive power for the frames was provided by a horse gin — a horizontal wheel 27 ft in diameter to which six horses were harnessed and as the horses walked round in circles so the wheel turned. This mill was destroyed by fire in 1781 and was then rebuilt to incorporate a Boulton and Watt steam engine. The rebuilt mill, too, has vanished.

Soon after completing his horse-powered Nottingham factory Arkwright formed a partnership with Samual Need and Jedediah Strutt who had already made a fortune from his invention of a machine for making hosiery. Strutt lived in Derby and was familiar with John Lombe's silk mill and the advantages of water power over the limited power of the horse gin. The three partners chose a site for their next mill at Cromford, fourteen miles north of Derby; it offered them all the advantages they looked for — there was an adequate supply of fast moving water in Bonsall Stream, supplemented by an artificial stream called Meer Sough which drained the adjacent lead mines and hence did not freeze in winter — the area was sufficiently remote to be safe from the Lancashire machine-wreckers — and the existing lead workings employed the local men, leaving the women and children under-employed.

The 'Old Mill' at Cromford was completed in 1771 and still exists, albeit

14 Old Mill, Cromford, England, 1771. With its top floor missing and replaced with an asbestos-cement roof, this is the original building in which Arkwright and Jedediah Strutt first powered cotton spinning by waterwheel (Photo – Valerie Winter)

extensively altered, with its top floor removed and re-roofed in asbestos; it is used as a colour works and looks generally neglected. Visiting the Old Mill now, it is difficult to imagine what a great leap forward it must have been, this first cotton spinning mill worked by water power, for it required the inventive genius of Strutt and Arkwright before all the technical problems could be overcome and the enterprise brought to success.

Arkwright settled near his factory, and under his paternal eye Cromford became the first of the company towns. Two hundred people worked in the Old Mill; they were mostly women and children who worked in two shifts of twelve hours each. Perhaps it is the thought of the five-year-olds toiling through the night, perhaps it is the sombre character of the Old Mill itself, but somehow there is a grimness about the place which is not found in Strutt's mills at Belper, nor in David Dale's in New Lanark. In 1777 a further mill was added at Cromford which survived until destroyed by fire in 1890, and in 1783 a six-storey mill was built a few hundred yards away on the Derwent itself, called Masson Mill, an elegant piece of red-brick Georgian architecture, the central part of which still exists in a mutilated form. With the completion of Masson Mill, Arkwright's Cromford Mills employed a thousand people.

Whilst the Cromford Mills were under the personal surveillance of Arkwright, the Belper Mills which followed were largely the creation of his partner, Jedediah Strutt. It is difficult to love the unyielding figure of Arkwright, but Strutt impresses as a man of high principle, concerned with his work-people and ceaselessly working for all the liberal causes of the day. Belper is on the Derwent, midway between Arkwright's home at Cromford and Strutt's at Derby, and here the first mill was built in 1776. It had brick walls and internal timber framing and was the first stage of a great milling complex which still exists, although the original building was destroyed in 1811. As long as the motive power was derived from the drop in level of a river, so there was a limit to the size of a mill complex, for there was a limit to the amount of power that could be generated. So, only a year after he had started the Belper Mill, Strutt began to build another at nearby Milford which grew as another company town under his paternal eye. The Milford Mills were demolished in 1964, but parts of the structure are preserved by London's Science Museum.

In 1779 Cressbrook Mill, Millers Dale, was built by an Arkwright associate, burnt down and rebuilt in 1815. The new building still exists and must rate as the most beautiful of the Derbyshire mills — take away the industrial junk piled against it and you have a Georgian country house of noble proportions. While Cressbrook wins on beauty, nearby Calver Mill of 1785, is the most impressive: it is a massive six-storey structure of fine stonework, exquisitely put together in its remote valley. Adjacent to the

15 Cressbrook Mill, Millers Dale, England, 1815; most beautiful of the early Derbyshire mills. Bell towers were common on the early mills to call people to work. The top floor windows are original (Photo – Eric de Maré)

mill is the wheel house, a stone building with the mountings of the two great iron wheels that powered the mill. The wheels themselves were removed for scrap during the war, but the structure still tells eloquently of the power generated by the tumbling Derwent.

The year before Calver Mill was built saw the construction of two other

16 Wheel House, Calver Mill, Derbyshire 1785. The wheels were removed for scrap during the Second World War, but the building that housed them remains (Photo – Eric de Maré)

fine mills which still exist: Samuel Greg's Quarry Bank Mills at Styal, Cheshire, now in the keeping of the National Trust so at least one early mill will be saved for posterity; and the White Cross Mill at Caton, Lancashire, extensively repaired after a fire in 1838 and now owned by Storey's of Lancaster.

17 and 18 Quarry Bank Mill, Styal, Cheshire, 1784. A beautiful mill now the property of Britain's National Trust (Photos – Eric de Maré)

17

19 White Cross Mill, Caton, Lancashire, England, built 1784. Extensively rebuilt 1838. The cast iron windows are original (Photo – Eric de Maré)

Early mills in Scotland

Arkwright's water-frame made him a fortune and he jealously guarded the patent. There were many who sought ways of using the water-frame without having to make Arkwright a partner in the enterprise, and in 1779 James Kenyon built a mill at Rothesay. He brought in some of Arkwright's former employees and managers and trusted to the remoteness of the location to dodge Arkwright's vigilance; it was Scotland's first cotton mill, two floors

20 Dean Village, Edinburgh. Traditional Scottish industrial building before the arrival of Arkwright in 1783 (Photo - Eric de Maré)

21 and **22** New Lanark, Scotland, 1785–1810. Scene of Robert Owen's social experiments, the mills are deserted now, but the housing, some of which can be seen to the right, through the arch, has recently been restored (Photos – Valerie Winter)

21

high, 42 ft by 13 ft, and much of it still exists. The waters of Loch Fad were harnessed to turn the water wheel that drove a thousand spindles, but Kenyon's cunning was not rewarded with great profits, and he sold the mill when Arkwright's own Scottish mills started production in 1785.

Arkwright went to Scotland in 1783. He met the Scottish entrepreneur David Dale at Corra Linn Falls on the Clyde and declared that they would make it the 'nucleus of a new Manchester' and called it New Lanark. Soon the new mills were under construction — massive stone buildings similar to the earlier industrial buildings at Dean Village, Edinburgh — and by 1785 the first mill was in production. However, it was in that year that Arkwright's patent expired. So when he quarrelled with David Dale the latter was left in full control of the booming New Lanark Mills, which were operated by five hundred pauper children whose dormitory, like the mill, can still be seen. In 1799 forceful, idealistic Robert Owen became managing partner and married David Dale's daughter Caroline. Owen was a believer in scientific management and a most successful businessman. He devoted his energy to building up a model community: he built a school for the pauper children, employing no one under ten years old in the mill; he introduced learning and music to all the mill hands and was a benevolent father to the settlement, which by 1816 boasted eleven water wheels and a population of 2297, of whom 1700 worked in the mill. However, as is so often the lot of social reformers, Owen made enemies — first of his partners who thought his social experiments might minimize profits and who did not like the agnosticism taught in his school; then of the women, who loved the bright houses he built for them, but were not so delighted with his regular inspections for cleanliness; and finally he alienated the workmen by his system of 'silent monitors' — coloured boxes hung above each man's workplace, white for excellent, black for dreadful, with blue and yellow in between, according to how hard each man worked; in comparison Arkwright's system of pecuniary perks and forfeits seems quite human. In 1825 Owen left for America and New Lanark stands today almost exactly as he left it, the houses carefully restored, the factories deserted and curiously lovely.

Another great work of Arkwright the tycoon is Stanley Mill on the Tay built in 1785 for Dempster, Graham and Arkwright. Here three tunnels, each eight hundred feet long, brought water to turn wheels generating no less than four hundred horsepower. These waterworks have been altered but they still exist and still generate power.

Fairbairn, pioneer of iron framed mills, was equally a great builder of waterwheels, and his most dramatic were installed at Catrine, Ayrshire, in 1827. Two cast iron wheels, each 50 ft diameter and 10 ft wide, generating two hundred and fifty horsepower, provided the power for a pair of large mills for a hundred and twenty years without a break.

23 William Strutt's North Mill at Belper, England, 1803. The fourth iron framed building ever built, this mill had an elaborate heating system worked by hot air ducted from a central heating plant (Photo – Valerie Winter)

Fire-proof watermills

The first fire-proof mills were steam mills (Chapter 3, p. 45), but the finest of the early fire-proof mills is the water-powered North Mill at Belper.

When Jedediah Strutt's Belper Mill of 1786 was burnt down in 1803, his son, William, immediately rebuilt it with an iron skeleton and this mill is still used by the English Sewing Cotton Co. Ltd, inheritors of both the Strutt and the Arkwright businesses. William Strutt had hesitated for a long time about the advisability of using iron beams, but a visit from his

24 and 25 Stanley Mill, Stonehouse, England, built in 1813 on the river Frome. Marvellous exterior of brick and stone, very simply used, equally splendid cast iron interior which is not at all simple (Photos – Eric de Maré)

24

friend, Charles Bage, who had successfully used them in a Flax Mill in Shrewsbury, convinced him and, once convinced, William Strutt moved with complete confidence: the North Mill at Belper is the most beautiful and most technically perfect mill of the time. Cast iron columns support cast iron beams spanning 9 ft, and brick arches span the 7 ft between the beams while each 7 ft bay has central heating, mechanical ventilation, light and power. How many modern buildings can boast such an array of mechanical services? The heating was by means of a fire with a big iron hood, air passed over the hood and was ducted round the building, entering the room through registers which could be controlled to give the desired temperature. The top floor of the mill is a schoolroom — a reminder of the tender age of the employees.

25

Strutt continued to build lovely fire-proof mills, but both the Milford Mills and Belper South Mill were demolished in the 1960s. In the South Mill the beams spanned 17 ft and were thickened in the centre where the load is greater.

While cotton mills on the Derwent are of paramount importance in the development of waterpower, similar histories could be written of the woollen industries east of the Pennines or in the Severn Valley. Indeed the mills of the Severn Valley are exceptionally well preserved as the area did not prosper in the late nineteenth century so they were not rebuilt. The finest of them is Stanley Mill of 1813, built at Stonehouse on the Frome, which has the first cast iron frame in the south of England and perhaps the finest anywhere.

26 Mill at Limpley Stoke near Bradford-on-Avon; examples from the North and the South of England of stone buildings, probably early nineteenth century woollen mills powered first by water, then by steam engine (Photos – Eric de Maré)

27 Mill at Barnard Castle

28 Picture from an early nineteenth century book (Photo – Eric de Maré)

Soon even architects began to notice the mills, but, typically, it was a foreign architect, Schinkel from Berlin, who first came to admire. In 1823 the German, Beuth, was in Manchester and he wrote to Schinkel, 'The miracles of the new age, my friend, are the machine and the buildings for it, called factories. Such a thing is eight or nine storeys high, has sometimes as many as forty windows along the front and normally four to the side. Each storey is twelve feet high, vaulted throughout the whole length, the span being nine feet. The columns are of iron, so are the beams on top of them. However, the walls are like playing cards, in the second floor they are not even two and a half feet thick. It is said that a gale blew down such a house before it was finished. That may be so, but without exaggeration about a hundred have been standing here for forty or fifty years and they still stand as in the beginning.' Three years later Schinkel came to see for himself and wrote of Manchester, 'Here are buildings, seven or eight storeys high, as big as the Royal Palace in Berlin — they are vaulted and fire-proof.' Is it too much to imagine that something of the early mills shows in Schinkel's neo-classical buildings, and through them to the work of his disciple, Mies van der Rohe, and thence to the buildings of today?

Early mills in the United States

Sam Slater, who had been employed in Strutt's first Belper Mill, built the first American cotton mill in 1793 on the Blackstone River at Pawtucket, Rhode Island, and the building is still in existence. Unfortunately, Slater left England just before William Strutt built his first fire-proof mill and the Pawtucket Mill is timber throughout, except for stone foundations and wrought iron ties in the roof trusses.

Early settlers had taken to America the heavy timber building methods of Elizabethan England and most early American building consisted of a heavy timber frame with clapboard siding. Invention of the nail-making machine in 1777 and the circular saw in 1814 enhanced the economy of wood and America is still a timber building country. The invention in 1833 of the balloon frame — a building method by which the heavy frame with its complicated joints is omitted and the load taken on light timber studs nailed together — proved the cheapest way of building and holds supreme for domestic construction, but the heavy load of cotton machinery and the requirement of open interiors without stud walls left the interior framing of mills in the old heavy timber technology. So by 1840 we have the situation where the cotton mills of England are the most technically advanced constructions in the land, but the American cotton mills are the most conservative of American buildings.

Typical early nineteenth century American mills followed the Pawtucket model; they were generally about 50 ft by 150 ft and two or three storeys high. In the hope of reducing the fire risk, the outside wall was sometimes made of stone, as in the 1812 Georgia Mill at Smithfield, Rhode Island. This mill was destroyed by fire and rebuilt in 1853, still using unprotected timber construction, sixty years after Strutt's first fire-proof mill.

It was the need to carry heavy loads, not just the wish to lower the fire risk, which made the introduction of the iron column inevitable. An early example was the Pemberton Mill at Lawrence, Mass, built in 1853 with brick outside walls, cast iron columns and timber floors. In 1860 Pemberton Mill collapsed, killing over two hundred people. The jury investigating the disaster placed the entire blame on the Eagle Iron foundry who cast the columns, and Charles Bigelow, the architect who specified them. It is therefore small wonder that subsequent mill builders were distrustful of iron and the water power era was over before America had a mill as sophisticated as the North Mill at Belper. The trouble at Lawrence was twofold, a lack of proper calculations and the American practice of casting cast iron columns horizontally so that the core mould could become eccentric and a round column might have paper-thin metal on one side.

Turbines

During the first half of the nineteenth century water power everywhere gave way to steam, but the use of turbines in the 1850s gave it a new lease of life.

Much of the work on the development of turbine drive for factories was done in France, and by the late nineteenth century much British industry was powered by French-made turbines.

Outstanding among the late water powered factories is the Menier chocolate factory at Noisel-sur-Marne designed by Jules Saulnier and built in 1871-2. Here four stone piers are built into the bed of the Marne and turbines built into each of the three spaces between them. Across these piers span four great iron box girders supporting a four-storey iron framed factory. The outer walls are brick but the entire load is taken on the iron framing, making it a very sophisticated structure for its day. Externally it is styled like the polychromatic buildings of Colmar, but the iron frame, complete with diagonals, is permitted to read on the facades; for while the builders of the cast iron mills had used supports styled like a classical column, Saulnier used straight wrought iron members rivetted together and took as his model timber factories such as the Gobelins in Paris where the frame was braced, not by brick walls, nor by rigid connexions, but by the diagonal members of the frame — a logical form to the metal frame which had frightened designers until the Hancock Building was built in Chicago nearly a hundred years later.

Nineteenth century turbines worked best when placed horizontally where there was a good head of water — not the ten feet or so typical of the English mill. So the most spectacular examples are to be found in mountainous regions. The Contonificio Feltrinelli Mill at Campione on Lake Como has a resevoir on the rop of an adjacent cliff nearly four hundred feet high and water at this pressure is piped around the factory to drive a separate turbine on each of the sixty-eight ring-spinning frames and the numerous carding and other machines.

3 Steam power and textile mills

In 1776 Boulton and Watt made their first steam engine, and within a year Arkwright was writing to them about the possible installation of one at Cromford. Nothing came of these first enquiries, but Arkwright remained uneasy with a state of affairs where the supply of water for his two water-wheels was dependent on factors outside his control, and in 1780 an eight horsepower Boulton and Watt engine was pumping the water from the tail race back into Cromford Sough, giving Arkwright control of his power source independent of the vagaries of the weather or the activities in the lead mines.

In 1784, the production of Boulton and Watt engines giving rotary power led to their immediate adoption at Albion Mill, and in 1785 Arkwright's competitors, the Robinsons, installed one to drive their mills in Popplewick, Nottinghamshire. The Robinsons' mills had been driven by a thirty foot waterwheel on the River Leen, but the flow of the Leen is unreliable, and was rendered more so by their upstream neighbour, Lord Byron of New-stead Abbey, whose hobby was to engage his servants in naval battles on his lake where he kept a twenty-gun warship for the purpose! Lord Byron was as mad about ornamental waterworks as about naval battles, so it is small wonder that the Robinsons found their flow of water doubtful, and were the first textile millers to turn to the reliability of the rotary steam engine. A parallel case of a landowner's water works forcing a mill-owner to install a steam engine is to be found in the novel *John Halifax, Gentleman;* in this case Mrs Craik had observed the installation of a steam engine at Dunkirk Mill, Nailsworth, Gloucestershire, and gives a vivid description of the first run of a steam engine:

He opened the valve.

With a strange noise, that made the two Enderley men spring back as if the six devils were really let loose upon them, the steam came rushing into the cylinder. There was a slight motion of the piston-rod. 'All's right! it will work?'

No, it stopped.

John drew a deep breath.

It went on again, beginning to move slowly up and down, like the strong right arm of some automaton giant. Greater and lesser cog-wheels caught up the motive power, revolving slowly and majestically, and with steady, regular rotation, or whirling round so fast you could hardly see that they stirred at all. Of a sudden a soul had been put into that wonderful creature of man's making, that inert mass of wood and metal, mysteriously combined. The monster was alive!

The coming of the fire-proof mill
Jedediah Strutt's son William took over the Belper and Milford mills from

his father, and as well as expanding the family business he was a practical scientist who lectured at the Royal Society in London on his experiments and became an FRS. These two aspects of his character came together in tackling the problem of the inflammability of cotton mills.

The early mills were a terrible fire hazard. Difficulty in transmitting power from the water wheel to the machines meant that the building had to be as compact as possible, and hence four or five storeys high. The mills had wooden roofs, wooden floors and inefficient ventilation; cotton was everywhere, overhead shafts were covered in oil and their bearings often overheated, lighting was by candle or open lamp and the entire mill was often staffed by five-year-old children and tired, overworked women. It is amazing that any mill was able to survive a week without being burnt down. Perhaps the large size of the timbers made it difficult for a fire to take hold. It certainly delayed structural collapse and enabled the occupants to escape. Casualties in early mill fires were surprisingly light.

In 1781 Arkwright's first mill was burnt down. In 1788 the Darley Abbey Mill belonging to William Strutt's brother-in-law was gutted by fire. In 1791, the year London's Albion Mill was burned out, no fewer than five Derbyshire mills suffered the same fate. Clearly something had to be done.

Mediaeval cathedrals had had a fire problem with their timber roofs which had been beautifully, but very laboriously, solved by constructing stone vaulting underneath the wooden rafters. The mill builders of the late eighteenth century had to look for more economical solutions, and turned to iron. Cast iron had been used in Europe for small items since the thirteenth century, and from 1600 onwards the production of cannon gave the ironfounders the experience they needed for the manufacture of cast iron columns for buildings. These were used in St Ann's church, Liverpool, in 1770 and their use rapidly spread to the mills. However, the construction of fire-proof floors proved a much more difficult problem.

In 1785–90 the Palais Royal Theatre in Paris was rebuilt with a wrought iron frame and hollow pot floors (hollow pots are like large bricks, made hollow to reduce the weight). William Strutt heard about it and tried to obtain drawings, but this was impossible at the time of the French Revolution and he had to be content with a rather inadequate description. However, Strutt would probably have seen the cast iron bridge built at Coalbrookdale in 1779, and more important, he was a relation of an ironfounder called Walker with whom he did extensive business. Walker was the man associated with the American bridge engineer Paine, who came to England to obtain the castings for a bridge he had designed to span the Schuylkill River at Philadelphia. Paine and Walker exhibited a hundred-and-ten-ft span iron bridge on Paddington Green in 1789, but the American War of Independence prevented the Philadelphia bridge from being built and its design was used for a bridge in Sunderland. In spite of all this knowledge, Strutt was cautious and did not venture to use iron for the beams of his first fire-proof buildings.

Strutts Calico Mill, built at Derby in 1792 and 1793 was 115 ft by 30 ft and six floors high. Columns were of cast iron, cruciform shape on plan to give the best structural shape without entailing the casting difficulties of hollow columns. Beams were of timber and the exposed underside was protected from fire by plaster and sheet metal; spanning between these beams was a vault of hollow pots, and the floor above them was made level with sand and given a brick tile finish. Similar vaults spanned between the lower chords of the roof trusses to protect the roof timbers. The Calico Mill was immediately followed by another Strutt building of similar construction — a warehouse at Milford.

William Strutt's Calico Mill and his Milford warehouse were fire-proof buildings, but the use of timber beams covered with sheet metal and plaster was at best an interim development. It now remained for a mill builder to take the next logical step and to design a mill with beams as well as columns of iron, and that step was taken by Strutt's friend Charles Bage, whose flax mill at Shrewsbury was completed in 1797, just six years after the Albion Mill fire.

Marshal and Benyon were textile manufacturers in Leeds and in 1796 their five-storey steam-driven mill was destroyed by fire, only five months after completion, and ten people had perished in the flames. So when these men planned a new mill at Shrewsbury later that year, they must have listened sympathetically to the ideas on iron construction of their new partner, Charles Bage. The building of the Benyon, Marshall and Bage Flax Mill at Castle Foregate, Shrewsbury, was left entirely in Bage's hands and he built the first building ever built with interior framing entirely of iron. It still exists and is now used as a maltings, the windows are blocked and it looks rather sad on the outside, but inside it is quite delightful and virtually unchanged.

Shrewsbury was the centre of the iron industry at the time, and Charles Bage was fascinated with what he saw going on around him. He corresponded with William Strutt and was fully cognizant of developments at Derby and Milford. When Telford built a cast iron aqueduct on the Shrewsbury canal, Bage watched with interest. It was on the data from tests carried out at Ketley Ironworks on the iron for this aqueduct that Bage worked out his theories for calculating the stress in his structures — to an acceptable degree of accuracy. The mill is 177 ft by 40 ft and five floors high, with an engine house at one end; no combustible material was used in its construction — staircases were of stone, windows were of cast iron. Internally there were three rows of columns, the centre row modified to

29 and **30** Benyon, Marshall and Bage Flax Mill, Shrewsbury, England, 1797. The first building in the world to have columns and beams of iron and hence the progenitor of all our steel framed buildings. The centre columns have a cap to take shafting to drive the machines. The building is now a malting, and two-thirds of the windows in the brick outer wall have been blocked (West Midland Photo Services Ltd)

29

take shafting, iron beams span between the columns; these beams vary in width in accordance with Bage's understanding of the stresses within them, and the columns are similarly fattened half way up to prevent buckling. The top floor is of similar construction, but as there is less weight there is only one row of columns, and the ceiling is raised in the centre to throw rain water to the sides of the building. This ceiling is brick vaulted like the floors below, and this gives the building its characteristic external appearance, for each vault has its own little roof running across the mill so the long

30

elevations are topped by a row of gables. The floor heights and the bay sizes vary according to the machine layout Bage required.

In 1802 Bage built a mill at Meadow Lane, Leeds. In the five years since designing the Shrewsbury Flax Mill he had learnt a great deal more about iron construction, and the Leeds Mill was much more sophisticated technically, but unfortunately this building, and a later Bage mill at Shrewsbury, have disappeared and little is known about them.

In 1803 an extension was added at right angles to Bage's 1797 Shrewsbury

31 Roof trusses to Charles Bage's 1803 extension to the Flax Mill, Shrewsbury. The oldest cast iron roof trusses in existence, the members are slotted together. The exposed timber roof would seem a retrograde step from the original factory, which had brick vaulting to the top floor (West Midland Photo Services Limited)

Flax Mill, and, strange to relate, this extension had wooden floors. The fates, however, were logical and in 1811 the extension was completely destroyed by a fire which left the original mill unharmed. Within six months this extension was rebuilt, in similar construction to the original mill, except for the top floor which is an airy attic in between the cast iron roof trusses, formed of castings which chinese-puzzle into one another without bolts or rivets.

The steam engine in the Shrewsbury Flax Mill had been installed by Boulton and Watt in 1797, so they had every opportunity to see the mill while it was being built. When they were asked to build a new mill for the Salford Twist Co. in 1799 they developed the iron frame for this very large mill, using hollow cast iron columns with flanged beams to support the floors. The building was heated by steam which was passed through the hollow columns, and in 1805 gas lighting was installed. The completion of the Salford Twist Mill in 1801 put a magnificent iron structure right in the middle of the Lancashire textile industry, and the use of the iron frame spread. When Hodgkinson made calculations reliable in the 1820s cast iron construction became normal.

For a while all seemed well, and there was confidence in the air. However, cast iron is brittle and can crack suddenly in the heat of a fire, especially if water is thrown on it, and settlement or overloading can cause a column to fracture without warning; disasters continued to happen, as at Lower-house Mill, Oldham, which partly collapsed in 1844 with the loss of twelve lives. In view of these risks, and for reasons of economy, many mill builders continued to use wood throughout the nineteenth century. The best wood-framed mills were built on the 'slow burning principle' as at Crest Mill, Castleton, where one-inch maple flooring is laid on joists (11 in. by 3 in.) touching one another to give a solid timber floor a foot thick. It would take a very serious fire to do more than char such a construction and it was probably the safest of nineteenth century mill floors. Abundant timber made such floors common in America, and the need to run belting or chutes through the floor in random positions led to similar floor construction in flour mills.

In 1843 Brunel built his first Atlantic steamship, which had a hull of rivetted iron plates on wrought iron framing. Wrought iron does not fracture as suddenly as cast iron and the construction of Brunel's ship was watched with interest by the factory builders. In 1845 William Fairbairn, greatest of the mill builders, built an eight-storey refinery building with wrought iron floor beams with thin curved iron plates spanning between them and concrete above to make a level floor. Tie rods, which had always been below the old brick vaults and hence exposed to fire risk, were placed above the arches in Fairbairn's building and therefore buried in the concrete.

The next logical step in the development of skeleton construction was to abandon the masonry outer walls. This step was taken by an American, James Bogardus, who described himself as an 'architect in iron' and developed the prefabricated glass and iron building, usually with Renaissance trappings. Bogardus built a factory on Centre and Duane Streets, New York, in 1849, which was five storeys high, the street facades being cast iron, with cast iron spandrels for rigidity. Duane Street was widened in 1859 and we do not know whether the side and rear walls were of iron or of brick.

To complete the story of the arrival of the iron frame we must include a building which is not a factory at all but is constructed as a mill. This building is the Boathouse in the Sheerness naval dockyard built in 1858–60 by the engineer, Colonel Godfrey Greene. He had employed the contractors who built the Crystal Palace for a previous naval building and learnt about iron construction from them. The structure at Sheerness is entirely of iron and includes rivetted wrought iron plate girders spanning 30 ft; the first H and I section beams — normal for steel building today — were invented by Colonel Greene for this building. Bracing against wind and other horizontal loads is by rigid connexions between beam and column. The modern framed building had arrived so perfectly that it is hard to believe that the Boathouse was finished in 1860.

Late textile mills

During the middle of the nineteenth century change in the English mills was slow and the American Civil War caused a shortage of raw cotton and a severe slump. However, this difficult period was followed by a new boom — and a new scale of operations. General use of the self-acting mule and the introduction of the ring spinning frame demanded a greater size both of factory and of investment, leading to ownership by limited liability companies and a more anonymous capitalism than that of Strutt and Owen who had lived by their mills. The Lancashire mills of 1860–1900 were built of hard, dark red Accrington bricks; shareholders had to be impressed by appropriate decoration and to see the name of the mill in large letters on the skyline. Typical of such a structure is Hawthorne Mill at Chadderton, between Manchester and Oldham, built in 1878 and little changed when visited over ninety years later.

Hawthorne Mill is an oblong building and rises to a height of five storeys plus a basement. The outer walls are of dark red brick and the inside framing consists of rows of cast iron columns, 10 ft 6 in. apart, supporting cast iron beams spanning 20 ft 3 in. which in turn support small cast iron beams, 3 ft 6 in. apart, with brick arches spanning between them. On the east side is a staircase, carried up above the roof to house the tank for the sprinkler system. Sprinklers, which automatically spray an area of the factory in the

32, (**33** and **34** *overpage*) Sheerness Boathouse, 1858-60, designed by Colonel Godfrey Greene. The ultimate in metal frame construction, probably the oldest building in existence to be completely iron framed and the first to use H and I sections **32** (Photo - Eric de Maré) **33** (Photo - Eric de Maré) **34** (Photo - Admiralty records)

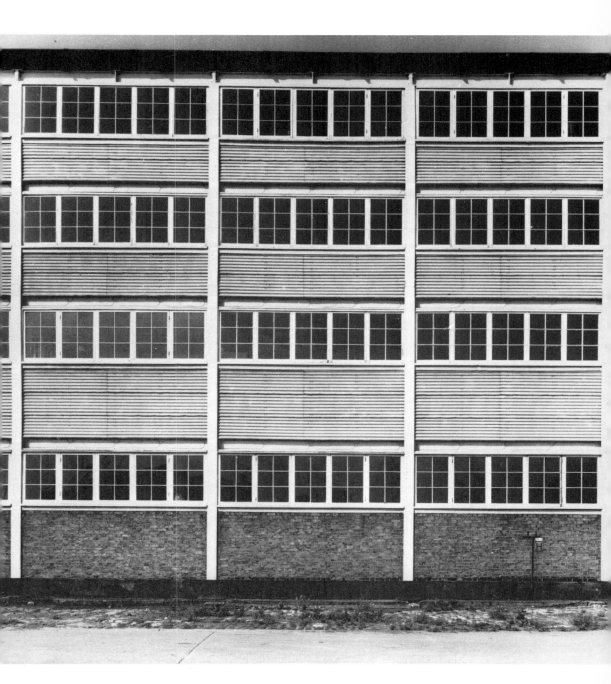

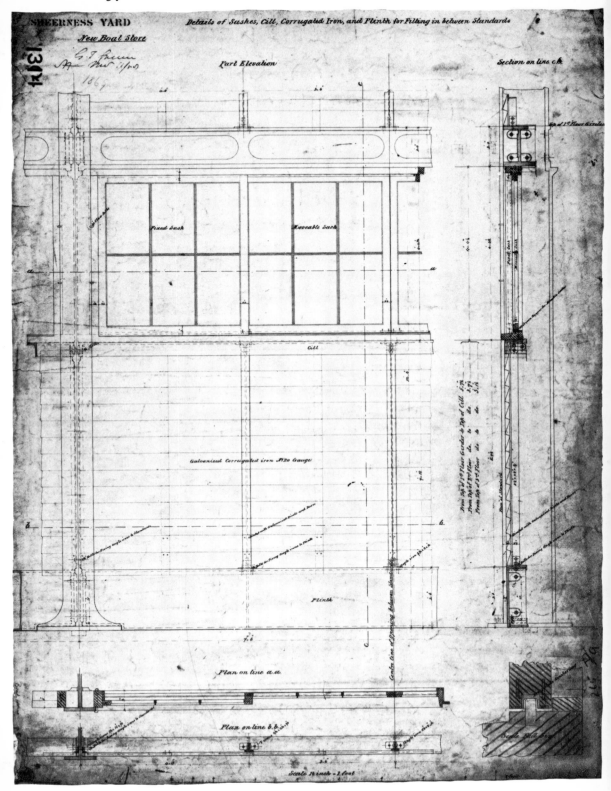

SHEERNESS YARD

New Boat Store

Details of Sashes, Cill, Corrugated Iron, and Plinth for Filling in between Standards

Part Elevation

Section on line c.b.

Fixed Sash

Moveable Sash

Cill

Galvanized Corrugated Iron N°20 Gauge

Plinth

Plan on line a.a.

Plan on line b.b.

Scale ½ inch = 1 foot

35 and **36** Hawthorne Mill, Chadderton, England, 1878; a typical mill of the period, still powered by the original steam engine, rope drive and overhead shafts. The projection with the two big arches contains the engine (Photos – Valerie Winter)

35

event of fire, had been in use for some time: early examples, as the Galgate Silk Mills of 1851, simply had a cast iron tank on the roof to supply water to the sprinklers. This caused problems in freezing weather and by 1878 tanks were incorporated in brick towers over the staircase. This tower at Hawthorne Mill is given a decorative roof and has the name of the mill built into the wall in white bricks so that it can be seen from all over the town. On the west side of the factory is a big room, its windows arched and mullioned like a nonconformist chapel of the period, containing the power plant, originally coal-driven but now converted to oil. The original 1878 steam engine still powers the mill and is in beautiful condition; built by George

36

Saxon, it is a four cylinder triple expansion engine developing 1250 horse-power, driving a 26 ft diameter flywheel built of cast iron and covered with timber. To the south of the mill is a large pool where the condensed but still steaming water from the engine runs along a stone trough and splashes into the pool to cool.

Early textile mills, such as William Strutt's North Mill at Belper, had used shaft drive and bevel gears for the distribution of power, and the early steam engines had geared teeth on the rim of the flywheel and vertical shafting to the different floors. But in the early 1870s rope drive was introduced to Lancashire from America for taking power up to the individual floors, and the great space occupied by the rope race was enclosed in brick to make a fire division across the mill. The great advantage was that power was transmitted by many ropes so that a breakage did not bring any of the machines to a standstill. Ropes were of cotton and $1\frac{3}{4}$ in. diameter. The rope race at Hawthorne Mill is a typical, if early, example: the great 26 ft diameter flywheel is grooved to receive twenty-eight ropes, ten of which drive the carding machines, and the remaining eighteen take power to the spinning mules on the four upper floors; the rope race in a very dramatic space, some 70 ft high and filled with purring ropes, each moving at some 4000 ft a minute and criss-crossed with light metal galleries giving access to the pulleys for maintenance. There is a pulley for each floor, and each pulley is on the end of a shaft hung three feet below ceiling level, and pulleys on these shafts drive the mules by means of leather belts.

The second half of the nineteenth century was a period of rapid growth for the American textile industry, and when Hawthorne Mill was built near Manchester, England, the great Amoskeag Millyard was spreading along the bank of the Merrimack river at Manchester, New Hampshire. Built in numerous stages between 1838 and 1915, at the time of its liquidation in 1936 it was the largest textile manufacturer in the world. A mile long and following the curve of the river, the buildings of the Amoskeag Millyard face onto river, rail and canal; most have cast iron columns and timber floors, and the outer walls are of brick with sash-windows, giving great continuity over the long building period.

The period 1880–1920 saw the last boom of the Lancashire cotton builders, and the mills of this period were substantially bigger than Hawthorne Mill, partly because the scale of business was increasing and partly owing to a desire to have all carding machinery on one floor. The layout, machinery and drive did not alter appreciably until electricity came into use, but modern structural systems superseded the old cast iron frame: in 1895 Horrockses built Centenary Mill at Preston with a steel frame and concrete floors. The factory for Rose, Downs and Thompson built in Hull in 1900 was the first English factory to be built of reinforced concrete; it was constructed on the French Henebique system. After that the use of reinforced concrete was inhibited in England by building regulations which were not relaxed for another decade, and by that time there were many reinforced concrete factories in Europe. In 1910 the Swiss engineer, Robert Maillart, eliminated the beam and built a warehouse in Zurich which was of mushroom construction. Even when brick continued to be used for the outer skin, the need to light the interior of the mill, which at this time was often 130 ft thick, meant that the brickwork had to be reduced to a series of mullions, as at Broadstone Mill, Reddish, and prismatic glass was often used to deflect daylight into the centre of the building.

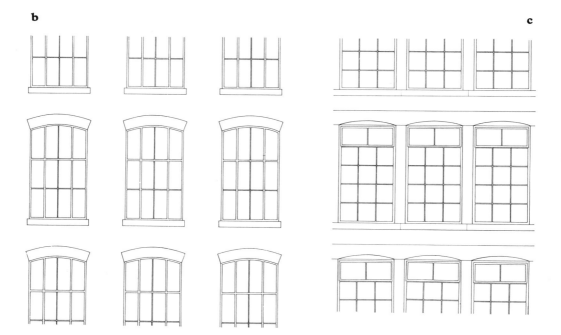

37 Window arrangement of typical cotton mill of each of the three main mill building periods, drawn to the same scale

a Quarry Bank Mill, England, 1784, typical Georgain windows and spacing

b Hawthorn Mill, 1878, the scale has almost doubled in the hundred years since Quarry Bank; bigger machinery and a deeper building meant that higher windows and more light was needed

c Broadstone Mill, Reddish, England, built about 1910. An even deeper building requires still more light, so the brickwork between the windows is reduced to a thin pier and there are now three windows to each bay of the internal structure

38 English Sewing Cotton Company's Mill, Belper 1912. Built adjacent to William Strutt's North Mill, which can be seen in the right of the photograph, the 1912 mill is typical of its period with closely spaced windows to the working areas and vertical circulation at the corners (Photo – Valerie Winter)

39 Mons Mill, Todmorden. As the name implies, it was built during the First World War and hence right at the end of a hundred and fifty years of multi-storey mill building in Lancashire, England. During this long development the windows in the brick outer wall grew bigger and bigger, so that by 1914 only thin brick mullions divided the windows (Photo – Eric de Maré)

These later mills were more highly serviced than their predecessors. Electric light came into use around 1900, first as carbon-arc lamps, then the early filament lamps followed by the introduction of Mercury vapour tubes in America which led to the daylight (more or less) fluorescent in use today. Heating was usually by steam pipes placed some eight feet above the floor, sometimes by air draughts drawn from outside and driven by a fan over gilled steam-filled tubes. Artificial humidifiers replaced the man with a can sprinkling the floor, for high humidity is essential in cotton mills to prevent static electricity firring the yarns. Dust extracts were developed, and in America the advent of mechanical ventilation takes us some of the way towards the totally artificial environment of some modern factories.

40 Mid-nineteenth century extension to Cressbrook Mill showing an early north-light roof. The internal construction was usually timber roof and trusses resting on iron columns (Photo – Eric de Maré)

41 Mills at Dover, New Hampshire. Typical American mill with double hung sash timber windows, brick pilasters and vestigial cornice

42 Amoskeag Millyard, Manchester, New Hampshire, USA seen across the Merrimack River. Construction is of brick outside walls, timber floors supported on cylindrical cast iron columns and flat timber roofs (Photo – Randolph Langenbach)

43 Upper Yard of the Amoskeag Millyard in winter (Photo – Randolph Langenbach)

44 Canal running through the Amoskeag Millyard complex, with the Lower Canal Building on the left and housing on the right. At the time of writing this great nineteenth century American mill complex is threatened with demolition (Photo – Randolph Langenbach)

45 Harmony Mills, Cohoes, New York. A great American mill with plenty of the styling one expects on a French provincial Hotel de Ville, and a statue of the founder gazing down at you. Manchester (UK) cannot compete with this!

Single-storey buildings

All the textile mills discussed so far have been descendants of John Lombe's Derby Silk Mill. However, for heavy industrial operations, as at the railway repair sheds at Swindon, the Victorians had developed the single storey, roof lit, industrial building, and by the 1850s this type of building acquired north light roof trusses, and was often used for weaving sheds. Sometimes the single storey building was an annexe to a high mill, as at the Great Western Cotton Factory, Bristol. Sometimes it stood on its own as at Low Moor Mill, Clitheroe, built in 1858, which has cast iron columns and timber trusses, a form of construction which became increasingly common. By the turn of the century the north light factory had grown to a great size, as at Cromer Mill, Middleton, a steam powered weaving shed, measuring 400 ft by 200 ft.

The decline of steam

The Victorian era was indeed the Age of Steam, and it was only in the last few years of the Queen's reign that other prime movers began to challenge the steam engine. In India the Bombay Manufacturing Company operated a diesel-driven mill, and Staley Mill, Staleybridge was powered by gas with equal success. But it was the erection of Acme Mill, Pendlebury, Lancashire, entirely driven by electricity from the supply authority's main, that brought the steam age to an end. A fair guess for the date of Acme Mill would be 1905.

Electric power gave a steadier rate of drive than had been achieved with the steam engine, giving an increased output in weaving of some fifteen per cent per loom, and this extra productivity meant that the spread of electric power in the textile industry was inevitable. At first individual drive to each machine was not favoured because small electric motors were both unreliable and inefficient. Some mill-owners powered the whole mill from one electric motor, which had the advantage of keeping the motor away from the dust, but kept the old rope-race. Others, as at Acme Mill, placed a motor at the end of each shaft, and because of the higher running speed the overhead pulleys were much smaller and the whole effect pleasant and light. Finally, when the motors themselves were improved, each machine was given its own motor and the power distributed in the floor.

4 The factory and the modern movement in architecture

The factories of the late eighteenth and early nineteenth centuries were the work of practical men requiring well functioning buildings and they chose their aesthetic canons to accord with this need. In 1755 the treatise of the French architectural writer, Abbé Laugier, was published in England; he advocated simple, unadorned structures of posts, beams and a roof because that was how man built before architecture became contaminated with the notion of style. One can imagine that these ideas had both an intellectual and a practical appeal to the early mill builders, who all seemed to have a puritan streak in them — and so the style was set for over a hundred years.

In the early years of this century, when architects were reacting against the historical revivals of the Victorians and the curvaceous caprices of Art Nouveau, they sought their imagery in the new construction methods of steel and concrete and in the function of the building to be designed. This brought them to a position where they could approach the industrialist, not as someone to put trimmings onto an engineer's building, but as people with a viewpoint very similar to the industrialist himself. A meeting of the ways had become inevitable and it happened in Germany in 1907 when the AEG electrical firm asked the architect Peter Behrens to design buildings and products for them.

The AEG and Peter Behrens

Peter Behrens started life as a painter, but in 1898 he began to design for industrial production — a rare interest for a painter at that time. He then studied architecture and in 1907 he met Herr P. Jordan, managing director of the AEG. Industrialization in Germany was barely thirty years old, and the electrical industry in particular was new, energetic and full of ideas; Jordan asked Behrens to design products for AEG — the packaging, the advertising and the buildings — in short to give the company what we would now call a 'corporate image', an unheard of step in 1907. In 1909 the AEG Turbine Factory was completed in Berlin. Often claimed as the 'first modern building' it is of immense size, the sides are glass, sloping inwards as they rise, and the structure is of steel and concrete used in a very direct way, but with a slightly self-conscious monumentality that was new to industrial building.

What could be more appropriate to mark the meeting of architecture and industry than a steel Parthenon?

The Fagus-Fabrik and Walter Gropius

Walter Gropius was a young assistant in Peter Behren's office when the AEG Turbine Factory was built, and he saw that German industry was alive and open to new ideas, but non-industrial architecture offered no commissions to a modern architect.

46 AEG Turbine Factory, Berlin, 1909, by Peter Behrens who was the leading German architect of the time and designed the products and advertising for the AEG as well as their buildings

47 Fiat factory built near Turin in 1927 with a testing track on the roof. Each part of the factory could be visited by car

When Gropius was twenty-eight, Karl Benscheidt of the Fagus Shoe Last company asked him and Adolf Meyer to design their new factory at Alfeld an der Leine. The result is very acceptable today when we see glassy buildings all around us, but it must have been absolutely stunning in 1911. Steel framed buildings had been built before, but they had been sufficiently heavy for eyes used to masonry construction to feel that they were safe — even the Turbine Factory had massive concrete corners to give it a feeling of solidity — but at the Fagus factory there was only glass at the corners, for Gropius said that 'the role of the walls becomes restricted to that of mere screens stretched between the upright columns of the framework to keep out rain, cold and noise'. This early attempt to express the lightness of skeleton construction by using whole walls of glass was more than other architects and critics could take, and for some years publications sympathetic to Gropius did not show pictures of the glassy parts of the building — people simply would not believe it! Yet to us it still has hangovers from the older techniques, that yellow brick cladding for example, or the way the steel cheeks at the sides of the windows slope outwards — a stylistic kick borrowed from the Turbine Factory.

Two years after the completion of this factory, Gropius published pictures of American grain silos, which, he said, 'can stand comparison with the constructions of ancient Egypt'. Architects, who a decade before had considered industrial buildings as beneath contempt, were now looking at them with wonder, as an example of rational thought, and as a new world of forms to explore.

Futurism, the Fiat works and Matte Trucco

Futurism was an art movement concerned with speed, and Antonio Sant'-Elia's drawings of the Futurist city show great buildings linked at many levels by transportation systems carrying lifts, cars, trains and conveyors, all in a state of frantic movement.

No Futurist building was built, but when Senator G. Agnelli of Fiat and his architect Matte Trucco built the factory at Lingotto near Turin in 1927, it was obvious that the Futurist vision of movement had come a long way from the young Bohemians who had thought up the ideas. The Fiat factory is large, three and a half million square feet of factory, where steel windows and concrete construction of the most sophisticated and beautiful kind were mixed up with mouldings and other left-overs from the classical architecture that the Futurists had been reacting against. The layout of the factory is such that materials enter at ground floor level, cars are made in a continuous assembly line which extends from floor to floor by great spiral ramps and the completed cars emerge at roof level onto a testing track one and a half miles long, eighty feet wide and seventy feet above the ground! It seems

48 Fromm Rubber Factory, Berlin, built in 1930 by Arthur Korn; it is the first building to take the clear expression of the metal frame beyond that of the Sheerness Boathouse

that the Futurists love of the movement of cars was shared by the more affluent Italians who actually owned them — for Agnelli had the factory planned so that he and his colleagues could drive round and see every machine without stepping out of their cars! Forty years later, the Americans have not taken the 'drive-in' principle so far.

The Van Nelle Factory and Brinkman and Van der Vlugt

The Van Nelle tobacco and cocoa factory was built in Rotterdam between 1928 and 1930 by the Dutch architects, Brinkman and Van der Vlugt, and their assistant, Mart Stam. The main block can be seen as the culmination of the multi-storey framed factory which had steadily developed without fundamental change since the Derby Silk Mill.

The owners' statement that 'no kind of decoration is used anywhere, as it is held to have an adverse effect upon the workers' shows the mood of the time, and how owner and architect shared a common viewpoint. Architecturally magnificent, it followed only three years after the Bauhaus building and carried through a complex programme with originality and total architectural consistency.

Fromm Rubber and Arthur Korn

The Fagus factory was built largely of brick, Fiat and Van Nelle of reinforced concrete, and in terms of the development of light machine-made structures these buildings were a retrogressive step from the Sheerness Boathouse. The development of the metal frame was taken up enthusiastically by Arthur Korn who, with S. Weitzmann, designed a factory in 1930 which was a celebration of the steel frame and went far beyond the Boathouse. The three-storey-high part of this Berlin rubber factory was supported on a steel frame, clearly expressed and painted bright red: infil was of white glazed brick and steel windows imported from England. The rectangular bays of the clearly expressed frame give the building its character, and this imagery was developed by Mies van der Rohe in Chicago a decade later.

The Boots Factory and Sir Owen Williams

In 1930 the English were isolated from the architectural ferment going on in Europe, and it took an engineer to show them what could be achieved by the new architecture on a grand scale. The Boots Factory at Beeston, near Nottingham, designed by Sir Owen Williams, is still a splendid building to see, but visitors in 1932 simply could not believe their eyes when they saw the great mushroom columns and the great areas of glass handled with complete assurance and a total absence of architectural styling. The *Architects' Journal* of the day referred to 'a factory totally new, both in design

and construction . . . . it is impossible to impart but the faintest conception of the novel methods of construction which manifest themselves everywhere. It is designed with scientific precision; it is a building of law and order in planning, construction and working; a building brought about by the very essence of method.'

Reinforced concrete mushroom columns, similar to those at Van Nelle, divide the building into 30 ft by 23 ft bays, and as the mushroom is a cantilever construction the columns are set in from the skin which is free to be entirely glazed; indeed abundant daylight was held to be so important that the interior of the building was opened up in a series of wells like a department store of the period.

50 Boiler house, Illinois Institute of Technology, Chicago, built in 1950, it was one of the first buildings on a campus designed by Mies van der Rohe (Photo - Valerie Winter)

Krefeld Silk, Illinios Tech. and Mies van der Rohe

In 1933 Mies van der Rohe completed a silk factory for the Vereinigte Seidenweberein AG in Krefeld. It consisted of a cluster of simple buildings with regular concrete framework and steel windows and it looks today much the same as it did when it was built. The buildings themselves are straightforward, perhaps even a little dull, for it is the relationship between them that is important; the buildings that comprise the factory are clearly separate, and on plan they slide past one another to form a courtyard which opens out to new spaces as you walk through — the germ of an idea that Mies worked up to perfection a decade later in the planning of Illinois Tech. However it is not the layout of that campus that concerns the historian of factories, it is the boiler house that heats it, for here, in 1950, on a tight budget, on a seamy slum-clearance site on Chicago's south side, Mies achieved a miracle. He took the steel frame and brick infil which Arthur Korn had used for his Berlin factory, and developed it throughout the campus into an eloquent architectural language which, to use Mies's analogy, could speak poetry in the buildings of emotional significance, and good prose in the boiler house. The prose was received loud and clear, for much of the best modern architecture, and most modern factories, owe their form to the regular black steelwork and buff brick of the Illinois Tech. boiler house.

The Sunila Pulp Mills and Alvar Aalto

Built just before the Second World War, the Sunila complex in Finland is not just a factory, but, like Saltaire eighty years before, it includes the housing and town facilities of the workpeople. However, in contrast to Saltaire it is pure delight, with houses scattered through the neighbouring forest.

Erected for a consortium of timber firms, the Sunila pulp mills are dominated by great brick-faced towers into which 30000 logs a day are fed by conveyors; from these towers wood flows by gravity through various layers of machinery until it is finally processed and stored in a long white warehouse on the waterfront. Aalto has a life-long concern to humanize the industrial situation — hence the informal planning, the ad hoc structure and the use of brick — decisions which cannot have been easy for an architect in the forefront of the modern movement at that time. In many ways Sunila is an attempt to evade the real problems of the machine by resorting to a handicraft tradition, but one has to admire the way the site is unspoilt, with great outgrowths of rocks and trees cropping out between the buildings themselves.

The US Navy and Ernest Kump

When the world situation started hotting up in 1940, the American Navy invested $150 million in the San Francisco Naval Shipyard at Hunters Point. Part of this vast programme was an ordnance and optical shop, a building for testing submarine periscopes and the rangefinders of naval guns. This building was designed by the architect Ernest Kump and the

51 (*opposite*) 52 (*overpage*) Ordnance and Optical Shop for US Navy, built at San Francisco Naval Base for testing the sighting mechanisms of guns and periscopes. Take away the bottom two floors and no-one would believe that it was a building of 1941 (Photos – Roger Sturtevant)

53 The Claude et Duval Factory in St Die, completed in 1951; it is the only industrial building designed and built by Le Corbusier (Photo - Valerie Winter)

engineer, Mark Falk. Naval guns are heavy — so great red-painted cranes move through the structure; but the work needs light — so walls and roof are of glass and rooms of cathedral scale are flooded with light. Only the concrete lower floors say '1941' in a building that in other respects seems to belong to the 1960s.

Duval and Le Corbusier

In 1945 Le Corbusier prepared designs for the reconstruction of the war-battered town of St Die in the Vosges. Le Corbusier was an architectural giant, but his proposals proved too much for the citizens of St Die who found it difficult to agree about the reconstruction of their town except for one issue — they did not want Le Corbusier. However, one man did; Jacques Duval asked Le Corbusier to rebuild his mill and then stood by him through all the setbacks of six· years of building, so that every chair, colour and plant is as Le Corbusier wished.

'Architecture is the correct and magnificent play of forms under the light', said Le Corbusier, and no notions of industrial method were allowed

54 The Brynmawr Rubber Factory was completed in 1951; the central space is roofed by nine large domes each 82 ft by 63 ft (Photo – de Burgh Galwey)

to efface what he regarded as more important values. Because he was a good architect, Le Corbusier has solved the functional problems of a five — storey mill as well as other factories of the time — but with an imagination unequalled elsewhere — light filters in through brise-soleils, a beautiful concrete frame supports ceilings painted in bright patterns, elegant stairs lead up to the roof garden — and what other architect would dare to suggest to his industrialist client that the main production space should have some of the workers on a gallery to make a more beautiful space? Most factory builders endow their buildings with a sense of meanness and economy, but here Le Corbusier has imparted his own belief in the nobility of work.

Lord Verulam and the Architects' Co-operative Partnership

During the Second World War Lord Verulam, head of Enfield Cables decided that his firm's new factory would embody the highest ideals; with remarkable foresight he selected as architects a group of seven men who had worked together as students before the war but who had no experience whatsoever of building. He commissioned them in the month the war ended in Europe, and as the young architects were demobolized one by one they pitched in so that the basic design was finished by the end of 1945, before post-war architecture in England existed. With Ove Arup as engineer, thin shell-roofs — the excitement of the time — were brought into the fray.

55 Vinegar plant for H J Heinz Co, Pittsburg, designed by Skidmore, Owings and Merrill and finished in 1952, it has blue glass in aluminium frames as infil to a black painted steel frame (Photo – Valerie Winter)

The Brynmawr factory is reinforced concrete, with the main production floor roofed by nine domes, each 82 ft by 63 ft, and the space under them remains to this day the wonder of postwar architecture, a magnificent space beautifully lit. But Lord Verulam had briefed his architects that the building should not be extended and that it should be fairly tightly designed round the Enfield Cables processes — and, alas for high ideals, Enfield Cables could not make a success of Brynmawr and the building was taken over by Dunlop Semtex who have extended and altered it in a most unsympathetic way.

Heinz Vinegar and SOM

Skidmore, Owings and Merrill gained a well deserved reputation after the war for designing the office buildings of major US corporations. They studied the office problem as Albert Kahn had studied the factory two decades earlier, but they were better architects than Kahn so the results were more powerful on the architectural scene. In 1950–52 they designed a warehouse and vinegar plant for H. J. Heinz and Co. in Pittsburgh, Pennsylvania, and they brought their know-how of office curtain walling to the factory world, fitted it with blue glass and hung it on a four-storey structure of black-painted steel — the elegance is taken right through the building by making the floors of open steel grating like the boiler room of a ship.

56 The Burgo Paper Mill, built in Mantua, Italy, in 1962 by Pier Luigi Nervi. A structure like a suspension bridge is used to roof a machine that needed an unbroken floor area 800 ft by 100 ft (Cement and Concrete Association)

The Burgo Paper Mill and Pier Luigi Nervi

Ever since the first factories were built, their users have been demanding bigger and bigger spaces with fewer and fewer supports: Arkwright had to manage with a post every seven of eight feet; by 1900 spans of sixteen feet were normal; and by 1960 seventy or eighty feet was considered a very good span. Then the Italian engineer Pier Luigi Nervi cracked the sound barrier with a clear span of five hundred and thirty-five feet! The building, which is in Mantua, houses a long machine which takes in logs at one end and delivers rolls of paper at the other and has to be capable of being extended sideways to three times its size. It was claimed that the machine needed unimpeded floor space 800 ft by 100 ft and so Nervi produced a suspension bridge, hanging the great roof from towers 164 ft high, and because the cables do not have the abutment anchorages they would have in a suspension bridge, the towers lean outwards and have extra legs for stability. Nervi claims that it was all logical and economical — one feels that a less imaginative engineer would have found an easier way, but that the drama would have been lost!

5 Ad-men, methods men and frontiersmen

During the inter-war years, factory design was looked at more closely than ever before and a new movement in architecture made architects sympathetic to the problem. A new industry — advertising — came of age and saw in the design of the factory itself a potent promotional device for the products made within; the organization and methods men studied the factory in depth to perfect the layout, yet the quickening tempo of technological change meant that buildings had to be adaptable to new requirements and new processes. Finally it was a time of unemployment and whole estates of factory buildings were promoted by governments as a means of bringing industry to distressed areas.

57 Marshall's Mill, Leeds, England, in the Egyptian style, an early example of a dressed up factory. It still exists (Photo – de Burgh Galwey)

58 Hoover Factory, Western Avenue, London, Perivale, Middlesex, a fantastic example of a 1930s factory given a treatment to impress the passing motorist. The factory has become its own advertising medium

Ad-men

The serious, puritanical outlook of Strutt, who admired buildings simply-built and unadorned, could not last forever, and when Sir Titus Salt had Fairbairn build his mill at Saltaire in 1857 his wish that his new town should have the best led him to ask the architects Lockwood and Mawson to style up the building in the Italianate manner (it was not easy, but they managed, hiding the chimney in a campanile). Green Lane Works, Sheffield, was given classical trimmings, Bow Bridge Mills, Leicester, had Gothic ones while Marshall's Mill at Leeds is Egyptian! In 1902 Voysey built an Art Nouveau factory at Chiswick for Sanderson's Wallpaper. Everything had been tried.

But all this styling had been for fun — or sense of decorum. Advertising was limited to putting 'Acmé' or 'Magnet' in white brick letters on the tower or chimney of a mill; the company's name hardly appeared as the owners saw themselves as people trading with the world, and the world did not pass their door.

The period between the wars saw a change of attitude: factories making nationally known branded products sought prominent sites on the new arterial roads around London or on the expressways of New England and erected great shiny buildings set in lawns, all floodlit at night and fantastic-ally styled to attract the passing motorist. Leaders in the trend were the English subsidiaries of American companies, as they had the promotion

85

59 Viyella Factory, Nottingham, England. A good straightforward factory with mushroom columns and all-glass walls, with the part round the entrance highly styled in stone. Note how dated this arty entrance looks, while the rest is still acceptable

consciousness of American business, but were not tied to existing sites like the parent company; good examples are Firestone Tyres on the Great West Road and Hoover at Perivale. The latter, designed by Wallis, Gilbert and Partners, is a fantastic composition, the centre part columned like a classical building, flanked by towers reminiscent of Mendelsohn's Einstein tower, and these flanked by a simple, four-storey concrete factory with triangular bay windows, all painted white but with bands of bright coloured tiles. As a contemporary description says with remarkable understatement — 'the building is situated in a prominent position facing on to a busy highway (Western Avenue). More money was spent on the front than was strictly necessary and it was carefully designed to create an impression which would be of favourable advertising value.' Wallis, Gilbert also designed the Pyrene factory on London's Great West Road, covered with 1930s ornament derived from the early buildings of Frank Lloyd Wright, and Wrigley's Chewing Gum factory at Wembley, designed to be seen from both road and rail. An extreme example, which takes us right back to Marshall's Mill, is Carreras' factory in Camden Town designed by the Collins and built in 1926. It had a highly coloured front elevation in the Egyptian style, apparently so convincing that the local guide said '. . . despite its exotic appearance the building is entirely British in construction!' More often the styling was modern and jazzy as at the Belling-Lee factory at Enfield designed by Donald Hamilton, or the Crown Cork building at Southall by A. L. Abbott; occasionally the modern styling would be quite sophisticated, as at the Berlei Corset factory by Brown and Henson or the Chicago Rock Island Railroad building by De Leuw and Cather, both with big curved walls of glass bricks — a real 1930s status symbol.

Sometimes the whole facade of the building would become a screen for advertising, as in the De Volharding Warehouse in the Hague by Jan Buys. Sometimes the styling may be modest to convey the image of a benign, efficient organization as in the Konsum Electrical factory on Kvarnholm Island, Stockholm, designed by Eskil Sundahl. On other occasions it may serve an idea of state, as in Professor Schmohl's Ullstein Printing Works in Berlin, Aryan Gothic in style.

It must not be thought that this concern with applied styling diverted energy away from the task of building efficient factories behind all the trimmings. Factories were better planned than ever before, and the Viyella factory in Nottingham, designed by F. A. Broadhead, is typical in having a beautiful mushroom construction, simply glazed on the outside, but the part around the entrance has artificial stone styling stuck on. Even Albert Kahn, arch exponent of the efficient factory, dressed up the bit on show; the Lady Esther plant at Clearing, Illinois, is a beautiful straightforward building, which changes to coy terra cotta and glass bricks on the side facing

60 Factory layouts by Albert Kahn; whether for cosmetics or the aircraft industry there is the same study of work flow. There are no structural walls within the main rectangle of the factory, so changes can always be made

Lady Esther Ltd, Clearing, Illinois

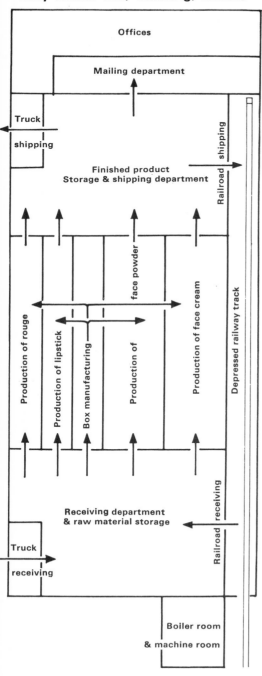

Pratt and Whitney Aircraft Company East Hartford, Conn.

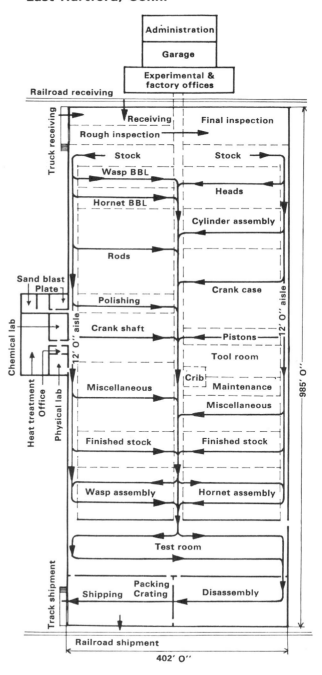

the road. However, Kahn's heart is not in it — his ornamentation gets simpler, so that by 1938 he is apologizing for the elaborate decoration of his Hudson building of fifteen years previously.

Methods men

The development of the multi-storey mill in the eighteenth century was an entirely British development which was adapted throughout the world. Between the wars it was the turn of the Americans, whose thoroughly methodical study of production flow and building costs made the old mills redundant and gave us elegant, single storey sheds, well serviced and with few supporting columns. Three firms of architect/engineers were responsible for this change, Giffels and Vallet of Detroit, Austins of Cleveland and Albert Kahn of Detroit. The greatest of these three was Albert Kahn, whose office, by 1929, was producing a million dollars' worth of building a week in the US and as much again in Russia. The *Architectural Forum* of August, 1938, said of him '. . . all that follows must be told against the background of these men who created the automotive industry. Henry Ford is their epitome. They possessed extraordinary vision to foresee new possibilities, they were willing to back their hunches with perseverance as well as money. When they came to the problem of housing the new industry they made great demands upon architecture, literally, if unconsciously, forced revolution in design, innovations in engineering, new techniques in construction. They were no less exacting on the architect. They wanted to deal with a businessman, they were profoundly suspicious of artists; they wanted fast work, no mistakes and flexibility to provide for inevitable changes in production. To all this they added a prime requirement of economy in first cost and maintenance. That these thoroughly materialistic demands have resulted in a series of some of the finest modern buildings, esthetically as well as otherwise, is Albert Kahn's contribution.'

Kahn's first factory was a multi-storey building on East Grand Boulevard, Detroit. Completed in 1903 for the young Packard Motor Car Company, it was the first American factory of reinforced concrete, and the first to have steel windows (imported from England). The combination of these two elements gave a lighter, brighter industrial building than ever before. This was followed by a factory at Highland Park, Michigan. Here, with a spacious suburban site and Henry Ford for a client, Albert Kahn produced a new kind of factory based on the requirements of mass production and the need for continual change in internal layout. To accomodate the continuous production runs, the factory was made all on one level, and since these production lines would inevitably change, the entire complex was put into one building. Kahn developed this design in numerous subsequent factories; all single-storey, they were lit from above; to enable the floor to be kept clear for machines, the lavatories, supervisors' offices and other

61 and **62** Factory for Lady Esther. A typical Albert Kahn plant of the mid-thirties, with the bulk of the building a beautiful workman-like box and the road elevation styled up to provide the right image for a cosmetic manufacturer (Photos - Hedrich-Blessing)

61

ancillary rooms were placed at a high level within the main factory enclosure.

The need for flexibility meant that the building was not too closely tailored to the initial plant layout but could be changed and extended — concrete gave way to steel structures with long spans and few columns. An extreme case is Kahn's building for Glenn Martin in Baltimore, which has an open floor, 300 ft by 450 ft, without internal supports. Later the necessity for natural light was questioned and some of the factories by Austins, such as the General Electric Company's building at Tiffin, Ohio, were fully air-conditioned and artificially lit. The technical problems were solved, although the psychological effect of the windowless factory is still open to question.

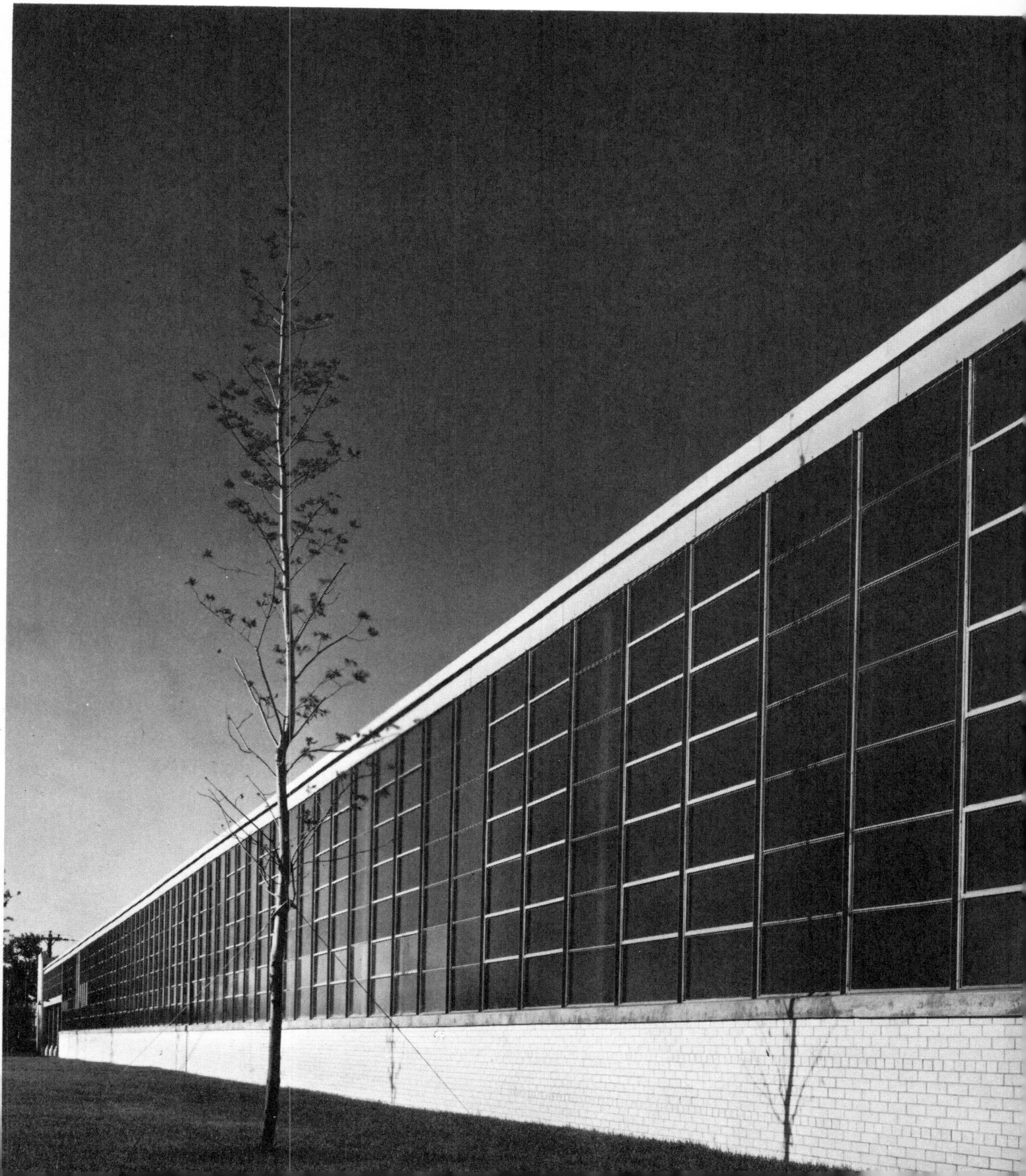

63 Diesel engine factory for General Motors, Redford, Michigan — a delightfully straightforward Albert Kahn building (Photo – Hedrich-Blessing)

64 The Export Building, Chrysler Corporation, Detroit, shows the characteristic
Kahn roof profile (Photo – Hedrich-Blessing)

65 Chrysler Half-ton Truck Plant, Detroit, showing the interior of a typical Kahn roof structure, with alternate areas raised and lowered to permit glass areas in between. The steel structure gives a 40 ft by 60 ft bay size and is part welded, part bolted (Photo – Hedrich -Blessing)

66 John Deere Foundry, East Moline, Illinois, designed by Giffels and Rosetti as a totally controlled environment. With no natural light, total air-conditioning and many aids to comfort, it is claimed that even the casting of steel can be carried out in a civilized place

67 Anthracite breaker, Locust Summit, USA. The straightforward functionalism of the frontier

Frontiersmen

While the high-powered methods men and admen were looking at the factory problem in the big cities, industry itself was spreading to more remote parts of the world and buildings were built by works engineers, often with great verve — as at the Anthracite breaker at Locust Summit in USA or the International Minerals and Chemical Corp. Ltd's potash plant at Esterhazy, Saskatchewan, both of light steel clad in asbestos-cement sheeting. However, these great buildings, for all their majestic charm, are a declining trend as the expertise of centralized organizations spreads to the furthest locations.

Planning

We cannot leave the 1930s without recording that it was a time of terrible unemployment which governments tried to overcome by sponsoring industrial estates in depressed areas.

Trafford Park Estate, Manchester, 1896, was the pioneer, followed by the Slough Industrial Estate of 1920. But it was the great success of Zlin, the new industrial town for Bata Shoes in Czechoslovakia, designed by F. L. Guhara, contrasted with stagnation of so much other industry in the 1930s, that impressed the British government and led to the 'Special Areas' Acts of 1937. Under these Acts industrial estates were built to bring new industry to areas of low employment. The best known is the Team Valley Estate at Gateshead, designed by William Holford, with factories on a grid of roads. This influenced estates all over the world, as at Dorstfeld West, Dortmund and Brook Hollow, Dallas. Other British examples are the Treforest Estate, Wales, by Sir Alexander Gibb and Sir Percy Thomas, the Hillington Estate by Wylie, Shanks and Wylie, bringing very small factories for light industry to Glasgow, and Queenslie, also in Scotland, by George Boswell, which is a period piece of Garden City planning, with crescents, fountains and brick buildings set in avenues — in great contrast to estates of the 1960s, such as Runcorn, by F. Lloyd Roche which is straight, square and metallic.

6 The cool, cool box

During the war, factories were rushed up all over the world — some of great size like the hundred-million-dollar steel mill at Fontana, California, which was built by Henry Kaiser to make the steel for his Liberty ships, or the Ford Bomber plant at Willow Run with its production floor $\frac{3}{5}$ mile by $\frac{1}{4}$ mile. But others were small and hurriedly built leaving a legacy of tawdry factory buildings. In Britain they were usually light steel structures covered with asbestos-cement cladding and topped with north-light roofs. In the late forties standards began to rise with such new factories as the ones at Stevenage designed by Leonard Vincent and the Sigmund Pump Factory by Yorke, Rosenberg and Mardell. In America the wartime black-out gave a great boost to the windowless factory; but twenty years later, although mechanical ventilation and lighting had become the norm, windows were reintroduced because people find it pleasant to look out. Big factories often have planted courtyards to make life tolerable for those working far from the perimeter.

68 Sigmund Pumps Factory on the Team Valley Estate, Gateshead, England. Completed in 1948 it was one of the first post-war British factories to look at the factory problem seriously. The building to the left contains offices and the high, monitor lit factory is to the right. Yorke, Rosenberg and Mardell were the architects

69 Processing building for Cooper Taber, seed merchants, at Witham, Essex. Designed by Chamberlin, Powell and Bon in 1955, this was one of the first English factories framed in black steel (Photo – John Maltby)

In 1952 two new industrial buildings were widely publicized — the Handkerchief Mill in Blumberg, Germany, designed by Egon Eiermann and the Dynamometer building at the General Motors Research Centre, Detroit, by Eero Saarinen. Both are framed in black painted steel and both have a precise industrial aesthetic derived from the work of Mies van der Rohe. Soon the influence spread, and many elegant, square industrial buildings were built. The cool box had arrived.

70 Cosmetic Factory at Morton Grove, Illinois, for Avon Products Inc. (Photo - Valerie Winter)

70-73 In the 1950s, Skidmore, Owings and Merrill were the pace-setters of clean, neat, beautifully put together industrial buildings. Here are four examples from 1957

71 Extension to factory at Tracy, California, for H J Heinz Co. (Photo - Valerie Winter)

72 Paper mill at Fullerton, California, for Kimberly Clark (Photo - Morley Baer)

73 Central Heating and Refrigeration Plant, Kennedy Airport (Photo - Valerie Winter)

74

75

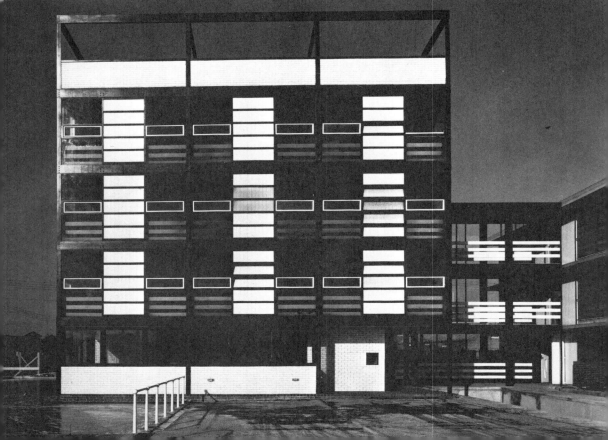

74 North side of a warehouse for CIBA Co. Pty Ltd, Lane Cove, New South Wales, showing simple concrete frame with concrete brick infil. Harry Seidler, architect (Photo – Max Dupain)

75 Adams Brands Ltd, Sweets Factory, Scarborough, Ontario, designed by Parkin Associates. Toronto architects quickly learnt from Skidmore, Owings and Merrill and by 1962 their standard of factory design was probably higher than in any other city (Photo – Valerie Winter)

76 (*below*) **77** (*overpage*) Women's Coat Factory for Barkin, Levin and Co. Inc., Long Island City. A very crisp factory designed by Ulrich Franzen. Note that the factory space has no windows and is a completely artificial environment (Photos – Ezra Stoller)

78 The York Shipley Factory at Basildon New Town, England, by Arup Associates shows the clean roof lines obtainable with monitor lighting when proper provision is made for all the service runs so that they do not clutter up the ceiling (Photo – Colin Westwood)

79 The cleanest box of all? — Storage building for Irish TV, Dublin, by Michael Scott and Partners (Photo – John Donat)

80 Most immaculate of English factories — Reliance Controls, Swindon, England, built in 1966. Team 4 architects (Photo - Norman Foster)

81–86 There is nothing quite like the boiler house for displaying the beautiful aesthetic of the black steel frame

81 Halsingborg, Sweden, Blasberg and Jais-Nielsen, architects

82 Cramlington, England. Chapman Taylor and Partners, architects (Photo – Valerie Winter)

83 Dordrecht, Holland, Maaskant-Van Dommelen — Droos and Senf, architects

In the 1960s, Myron Goldsmith partner in charge of design at Skidmore, Owings and Merrill took the steel outside the factory skin to give sun protection and to express the frame more clearly. Beautiful examples are **84, 85** and **86** (overpage)

84 and **85** show the Home News printing works at Franklin, Indiana (Photos – Hedrich-Blessing)

84

86 The Inland Steel building at East Chicago, Indiana (Photo – Ezra Stoller)

87 The Bath Cabinet Makers Factory, built in 1968 from designs by Yorke Rosenberg and Mardell, exploits the space frame for roofing, to give long spans without heavy steel members (Photo – Henk Snoek)

88 and **89** Factory in Bath for Rotark Controls. Here the architects, Leonard Manasseh and Partners, have let the shape of the space frame carry through to give form to the exterior. The entire roof was made on the ground and lifted up into position (Photos – Colin Westwood)

88

90 and **91** show beautiful crisp metallic factories in well landscaped sites

90 The Lignospan Woodfibre Factory, Otztal, Austria, designed by Stigler and Stigler

91 The SGS Deutschland Factory in Wasserberg, Bavaria, designed by Peter C. Von Seidlein

92

93

92 A progress photograph of the new Carroll Cigarette Factory at Dundalk, Ireland, gives an idea of the beautiful structure that can house modern industry. The deep roof structure enables a big span to be achieved without heavy beams and houses the ductwork for this air conditioned building. Architects, Michael Scott and Partners (Photo – John Donat)

93 Bigger spans and lighter roofs. Photograph of a model of new storage depot, Alexandria, New South Wales, with part of the roof covering removed to show the space frame structure which spans between columns 100 ft apart in both directions. Architects — Harry Seidler and Associates (Photo – Max Dupain)

94 Model of new Cigarette Factory for Players, designed by Arup Associates, has big clear-span production floor above service floors

95 The Petro-chemical plant at Stanlow shows one trend of modern industry — to get out into the open and not worry about buildings. It is easy to get rid of the gaseous by-products — but the downwind public is becoming more pollution conscious (Photo – Eric de Maré)

96 Dungeness Nuclear Power Station, England. The men give an idea of the size of a modern industrial plant and their white overalls tell of its cleanliness (Photo – Eric de Maré)

97 This power station in Los Angeles encases the plant in a frame to give staircases and galleries for access, but there is no enclosure. All right in Los Angeles — how about in Aberdeen? (Photo – Valerie Winter)

In 1949 Frank Whitney designed a plant for Blue Bonnet at Corpus Christi, Texas. It had no walls, just roofs and sunshades and the machinery on show. This idea was taken up again for power stations at Huntington Beach, Los Angeles, and at Willington, Derbyshire. The petro-chemical industry has built its great industrial complexes with the plant in the open air, with results that most modern sculptors might envy; in colder climates

98 '1000 ft by 2000 ft space', a model by Peter Pran, a student at the Illinois Institute of Technology shows the scale of space that modern construction methods can give (Photo – Hedrich-Blessing)

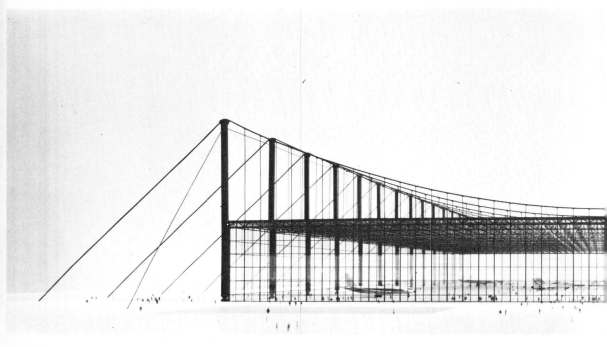

open air industry is not very pleasant for the maintenance engineer, but it simplifies the disposal of waste gases, as anyone living down-wind from an oil refinery will know all too well. However, as we become more conscious of the pollution nuisance we are less likely to allow industry to behave in this way, and we may see industry turning to the very big span enclosure for many of its activities.

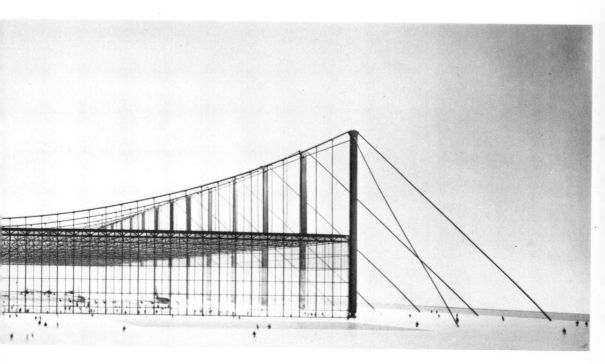

Selected bibliography

A History of Mechanical Inventions *A P Usher*, Harvard University Press

Industrial Archaeology Series published by David and Charles
   Lancashire – *Owen Ashmore*
   East Midlands – *David Smith*
   Scotland – *John Butt*
   Southern England – *Kenneth Hudson*

American Building Art *Carl W Condit*, University of Chicago Press

The Modern Factory *Edward D Mills*, Architectural Press

The English Windmill *Rex Wailes*, Routledge

The Functional Tradition in Early Industrial Buildings *J M Richards*, Architectural Press

Industrial Architecture of Albert Kahn Inc. *G Nelson*, Architectural Book Publishing Company Inc. New York

Short History of Technology from Earliest Times to 1900 *T K Derry & T I Williams*, Oxford University Press

The First Industrial Revolution *Phyllis Deane*, Cambridge University Press

Industrial Archaeology *Kenneth Hudson*, Methuen

Index